SILENT NODS, LOST DOLLARS

LEVERAGE PSYCHOLOGICAL SAFETY TO OUTPACE COMPETITION

RADHAKRISHNAN
SELVARAJ

ISBN

Hardcase 979-8-89519-556-7
Paperback 979-8-89363-870-7

Visual Designer
Sathyanand S
Head of Marketing, Logbase

Editor
Shashank SN
Founder of The Stupidpreneur

Book Cover
Haritha
ARTIST (National Athlete-Actor, Musician, Sound healer, storyteller)

Contents

Why This Book?

Psychological safety has been both a challenge and a revelation for me. It was a challenge when I did not recognize its importance, but it became a revelation when I finally understood its significance. This book is deeply personal as it reflects my own struggles to understand myself and my interactions with colleagues, friends, and teachers in various settings, including school and workplaces. Moreover, it encapsulates the observations I have made of those around me, such as children, adults, students, and professionals, as they navigate their own obstacles in life.

As a software engineer, my training and expertise do not directly relate to psychology or mental health. However, through my personal and professional journey, I have come to recognize the significance of psychological safety. This realization did not solely come from textbooks or research papers, but rather from real-life challenges. These challenges included struggles with self-esteem, conflicts at work, friction in team dynamics, and difficulties in understanding why people, including myself, behaved the way they did.

Through the lens of psychological safety, these experiences gain a deeper meaning, revealing patterns and implications that extend beyond the present moment. These are not fleeting issues; they have long-lasting impacts. The consequences of disregarding or nurturing psychological safety are significant and may only be fully understood after several years.

Understanding the concept of compounding, psychological safety has a profound impact, both positive and negative, on individual and group dynamics.

With this understanding, I invite you to join me on an exploratory journey. Together, let us delve into how the presence or absence of psychological safety can fundamentally shape our interactions, influence organizational dynamics, and, ultimately, determine the course of our lives.

For a long time, I have been a zero-sum player until recently, when I realized how it was hindering my personal growth. I see this book as a means to enable positive-sum games for many people, and I believe that psychological safety is one of the core components for effective collaboration.

A Respectful Approach to Real Stories

In presenting the case studies in this book, I want to emphasize that I deeply appreciate the efforts of the individuals involved. Their hard work and dedication are unquestionable.

My intention is to explore how, with the presence of psychological safety, teams and organizations could have achieved extraordinary results with fewer resources or avoided irreversible outcomes.

Every life is valuable and has the potential to create wonders when given opportunities. The loss of a life is immeasurable, and in some of the examples discussed in this book, we will explore how improved psychological safety could have potentially prevented tragic outcomes.

Please feel free to point out any discrepancies between the case studies I have presented and reality. I am open to being corrected.

The only outcome I expect from this book is that we will not repeat the same mistakes again.

The People Behind the Insights

I would like to express my heartfelt gratitude to Sahoo Manas, who conducted multiple sessions on psychological safety. The sessions held on this topic led me to a moment of realization, allowing me to connect the dots of my past and understand the underlying reasons for the challenges I faced.

And, of course, I must mention my wife, Vani, who has been an unwavering support system, granting me the time and emotional space to reflect and piece together the puzzle of my past.

Special thanks to **Vikrant Payal**, Senior Director at Epsilon India, who reviewed the first draft of this book and set the foundation for me to write the rest of the book, **Ubellah Maria**, Program management leader at Target, **Jagan Veeraraghavan** - Entrepreneur, and **Swaroop** my manager who have been a constant support throughout this journey.

Please Call Out Mistakes

You have put your hard-earned money to buy this book. I am grateful to you for choosing to try this book. I invite you, the reader, to actively engage with the content of this book. My intention is not only to share my thoughts and experiences but also to create a dialogue. If you disagree with something or have a better solution to a problem I've discussed, I would love to hear from you. This book is a learning journey, and I understand that I don't have all the answers.

Your insights and perspectives could provide valuable lessons for not just me but also other readers. Let's make this more than just a monologue; let's have a conversation.

Please feel free to reach out to me via email or LinkedIn. Your feedback and constructive criticism are most welcome, and I am excited to engage with you to deepen our collective understanding of psychological safety.

Email: krish.selvaraj@gmail.com

Connect with me on Linkedin

LinkedIn: https://www.linkedin.com/in/rk-radhakrishnan/

Who is the Audience?

If you think you've figured out every aspect of your life—be it personal, professional, or social—this book might not be for you. It is aimed at those who recognize that life is a constant work in progress; it's for the seekers, the curious, the ever-improving, and those who are open to examining themselves to see if what they do has second-order consequences or not.

The Ripple Effects of Psychological Safety

Psychological safety isn't confined to just one domain of your life; it's an ecosystem that affects your personal relationships, professional collaborations, and social interactions. Moreover, these areas are interconnected, each feeding into and being influenced by the others. For instance, a lack of psychological safety in your professional life can spill over into your personal relationships and vice versa.

The Cycle of Influence

The absence of psychological safety can perpetuate a cycle that extends beyond yourself. A person who hasn't experienced psychological safety may find it difficult to be a constructive team player. When such individuals find themselves in leadership roles, they can inadvertently create environments that lack psychological safety, affecting not only the professional but also the personal lives of their team members.

The Work in Progress

This book is particularly beneficial for those who understand that their emotional intelligence journey is ongoing. If you're striving to be a better spouse, parent, friend, team member, or leader, understanding psychological safety can offer invaluable insights. The term "work in progress" implies a state of flux, and that's the beauty of life. As humans, our perspectives shift, our knowledge expands, and our emotional intelligence deepens. This book aims to help you navigate that journey more consciously, equipping you with the tools to create and maintain environments—both at work and at home—where psychological safety can thrive. So if you're someone who believes that there is room for improvement, that you haven't figured it all out yet, then you are the reader I've written this book for.

Colour Images for References

Introduction

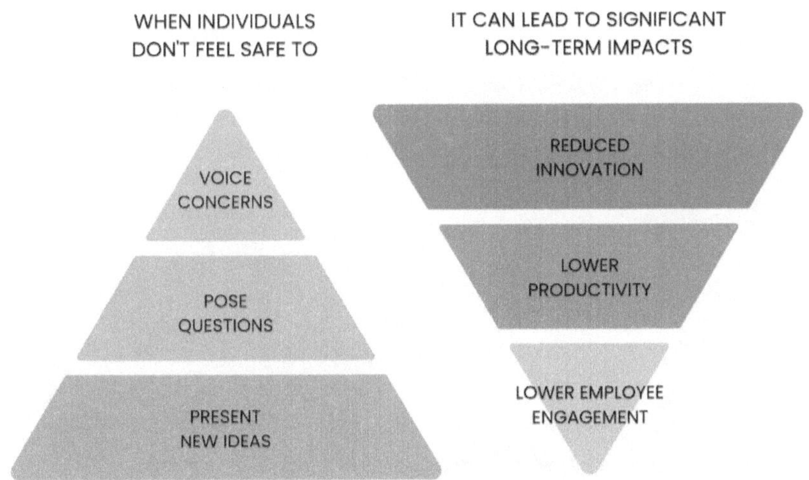

Voices Unheard: The Silent Impact of Psychological Safety

COST OF FEAR

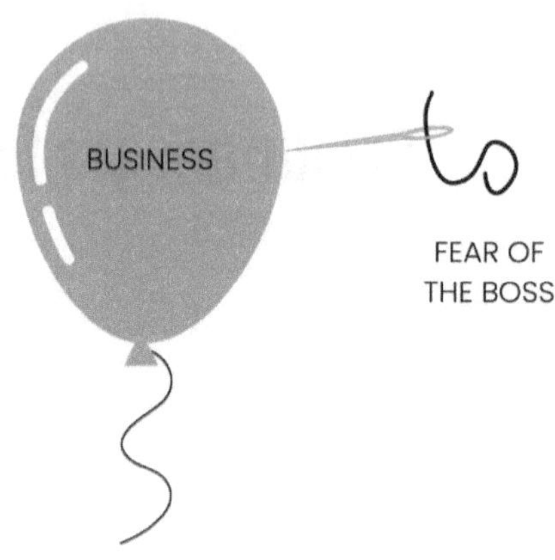

THE HEART OF PSYCHOLOGICAL SAFETY

FEELING **FREE TO EXPRESS** ONESELF – THOUGHTS, IDEAS, &
CONCERNS, WITHOUT FEAR OF NEGATIVE CONSEQUENCES.

The Power of Compounding: Lessons from Chinese Bamboo and Companies Like Flipkart & Infosys

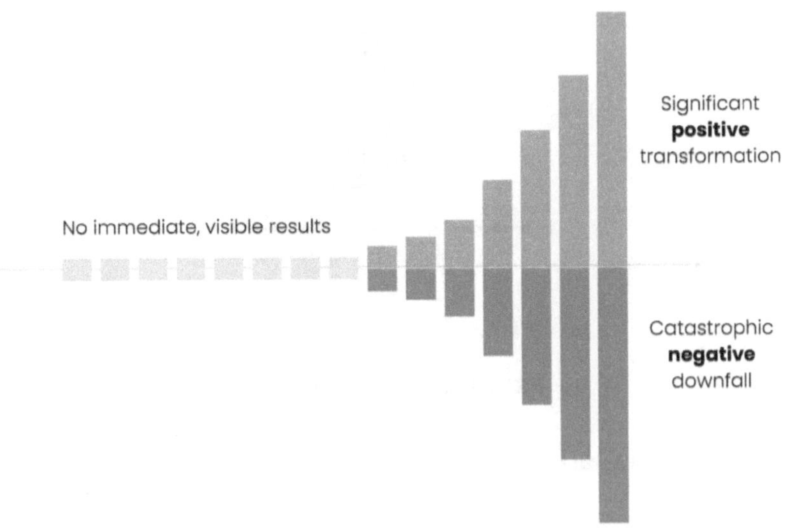

The Impact of Compounding in Psychological Safety

Intangible But Indispensable

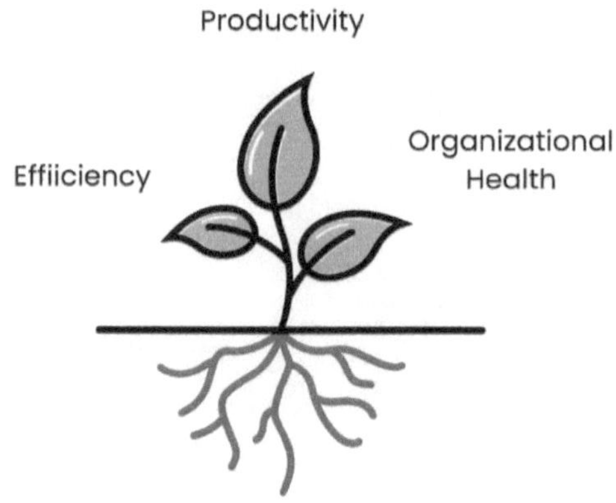

The Hidden Foundation

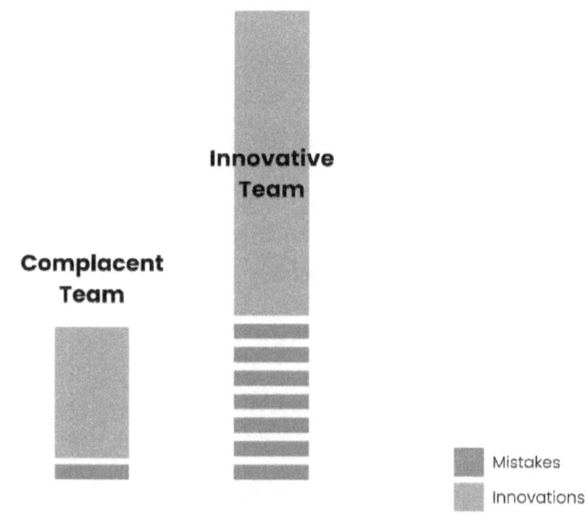

Better teams makes more mistakes;
And they become innovative.

A Cascade of Stress and the Imperative of Psychological Safety

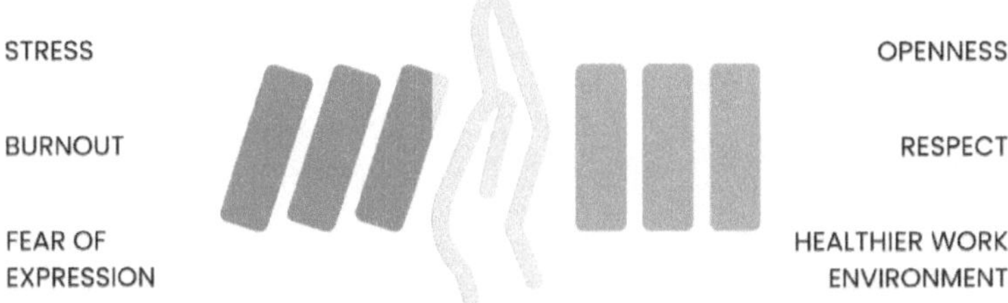

Psychological Safety: A Panacea?

Mum Effect

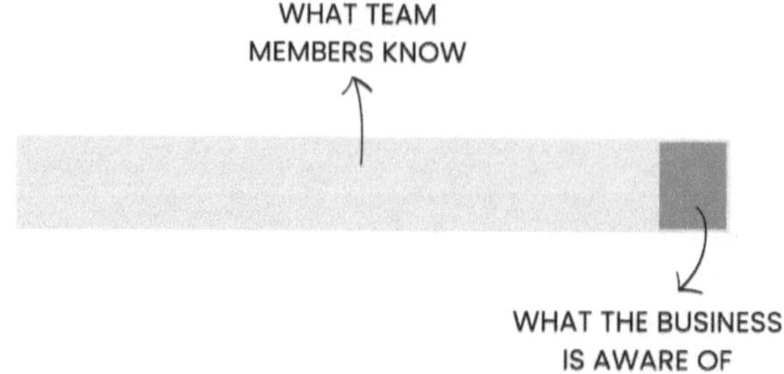

Team members know individually as time passes something is going to break.
But the business is not aware of it.

Psychological safety is not a **luxury**;
It's a **necessity** for thriving teams and innovative organizations.

Five Stages of Team Development

Psychological safety can ensure this information easily passed up the hierarchy and value can be protected

The Value Equation - A Hidden Multiplier at Play

Indications for a Business Owner/Manager to Find That There is Lack of Psychological Safety

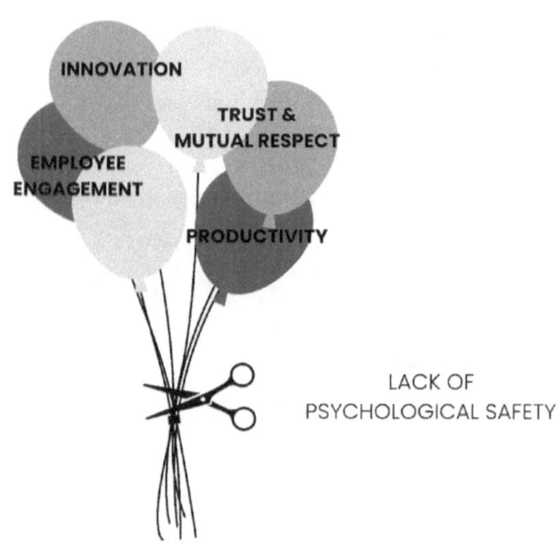

Rethinking Fear as a Motivator

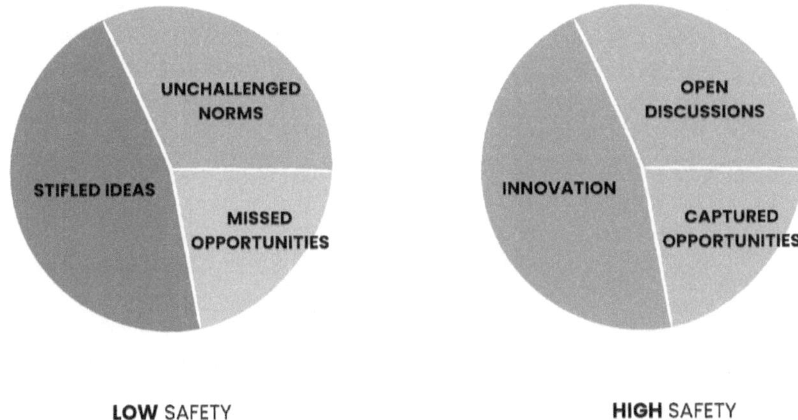

Psychological Safety - A New Competitive Edge and the Potential for Change

Introduction

Before we explore this, I want to present you with a few examples of what happens when there is no psychological safety in the workplace.

Scenario 1

Imagine yourself as one of the ground engineers for ISRO's first manned mission to the moon; during the launch, you notice a potential issue with the spacecraft's thermal protection system. You're torn between expressing your concerns, which might disrupt operations or cause unnecessary alarm, or staying silent. Knowing that the crew's lives could be at risk if your suspicions are correct, what would you do?

Scenario 2

Place yourself in the shoes of the flight crew aboard a domestic flight in India, traveling from Chennai to Mumbai. You're aware that the plane is dangerously low on fuel as it circles the crowded airport, awaiting landing clearance. Fearing that you might appear incompetent or unprofessional in the eyes of the airline's management, you're hesitant about communicating the severity of the situation to Air Traffic Control. Knowing that the lives of all the passengers and crew, including your own, hang in the balance, what do you do?

Scenario 3

Imagine yourself as a medical engineer at a leading Indian hospital, working with a newly imported radiation therapy machine. You've discovered a potentially lethal software bug that can administer excessive radiation doses. However, you're uncertain about voicing your concerns, fearing potential professional backlash. A patient is about to receive their first radiation therapy session with the machine. Knowing the consequences of an overdose could be fatal, how do you act?

Take a pause and think over these cases.

As you pondered over the above scenarios, it's worth noting that they are not merely a hypothetical situation.

In fact, very similar situations happened, and here's what happened in each of the real-life scenarios:

Scenario 1 (Space Shuttle Columbia):

The engineers' fears were, unfortunately, true. During the launch, a piece of foam insulation broke off from the Space Shuttle's external tank and struck the left wing of the orbiter, causing damage to its thermal protection system. However, this damage went unnoticed and unacknowledged during the mission.

When Columbia re-entered Earth's atmosphere on February 1, 2003, the compromised wing failed, leading to the disintegration of the orbiter. All seven crew members, including Kalpana Chawla, tragically lost their lives. Subsequent investigations revealed that some engineers had indeed suspected potential damage but were hesitant to disrupt operations or cause unnecessary alarm.

The Columbia disaster serves as a stark reminder of the grave consequences of a lack of psychological safety within an organization.

Scenario 2 (Avianca Flight 052)

The crew members, facing a cultural and language barrier, were unable to effectively convey the critical fuel situation to the air traffic controllers at JFK. They used terminology that indicated their situation but did not emphasize the urgency of their fuel state.

As a result, Air Traffic Control did not fully comprehend the severity of the situation and did not prioritize the plane for landing. Tragically, Avianca Flight 052 ran out of fuel and crashed, resulting in the loss of 73 lives.

The crash of Avianca 052 is often studied as a prime example that underscores the significance of assertive communication and psychological safety in high-stakes environments such as aviation.

Scenario 3 (Therac-25)

Despite being aware of the potential software bug, the engineers and medical staff failed to prevent the machine from being used. Consequently, six documented accidents occurred where patients received doses hundreds of times higher than intended, resulting in radiation burns and, in some cases, death.

This incident serves as a glaring example of the lack of psychological safety, which can lead to detrimental outcomes. It further highlights the significance of effective communication and prioritizing safety over concerns of professional repercussions in healthcare and other vital industries.

Now that we have seen examples, let us understand what Psychological Safety is.

Psychological safety is a shared belief within a team that it's safe for all members to offer ideas, ask questions, and provide feedback without fear of ridicule or negative consequences. This foundation allows for open communication, fostering an environment where innovation and constructive challenge can thrive.

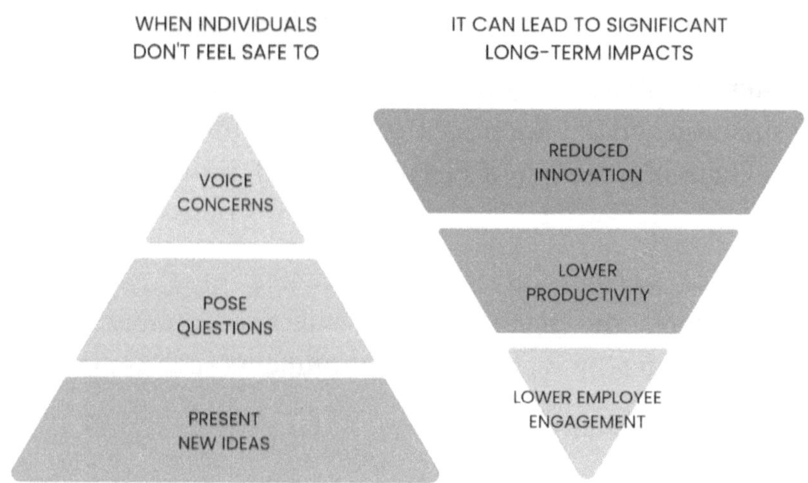

You might wonder how you can link Kalpana Chawla and her crew mates' deaths to a lack of Psychological Safety. The ground engineers who suspected the issue could have been scared of their manager or other repercussions if what they suspect ends up being wrong.

That fear of the boss is precisely what constitutes a lack of psychological safety. In work settings where fear is the dominant emotional currency, it's usually because team members don't feel secure enough to voice their concerns or ideas.

While some might argue that a certain level of fear ensures authority and compliance, this is a short-term strategy with long-term repercussions. True, you might see immediate obedience, but what you won't see are the innovative ideas, constructive criticisms, and proactive behaviors that can propel an organization to its full potential.

The issue isn't necessarily that the company will collapse without psychological safety; rather, it's that the company will likely not reach its highest possible levels of innovation and effectiveness.

Takeaways

Definition of Psychological Safety:

Psychological safety is a shared belief within a team that members can express their concerns, ask questions, and provide feedback without fear of being ridiculed or facing negative consequences.

Effect on Innovation and Growth:

Creating a psychologically safe environment promotes innovation, proactive behavior, and enables an organization or team to reach its full potential.

Scale and Impact Vary:

While the consequences of lacking psychological safety can be immediate and severe in some cases, in others, it may take longer to become apparent, but it is equally detrimental.

Personal Growth:

The fear of appearing incompetent can hinder individual learning and career advancement.

Activities

As a Manager, how would you establish protocols to ensure that all safety concerns, especially those that could potentially halt a launch, are immediately reported, and addressed?

- Implement an anonymous reporting system that allows engineers to voice concerns without fear of repercussions.
- Establish a mandatory review meeting before any launch where all team members must confirm the readiness and safety of the spacecraft.
- Create a culture where speaking up about potential risks is encouraged and rewarded, emphasizing the safety of the crew over the success of the mission.
- Develop a peer review system where multiple engineers must sign off on critical systems checks before a launch can proceed.
- Discourage individual reporting to avoid unnecessary delays and encourage team-based troubleshooting only.

As a Manager, what systems can you put in place to ensure that flight crews communicate critical information such as fuel levels without fear of negative judgment or repercussions?

- Develop a standard protocol that requires crews to report fuel levels to air traffic control under certain conditions, with legal protections.
- Train and empower all crew members to declare emergencies when necessary without waiting for approval.
- Institute regular psychological safety training that focuses on scenarios involving critical decision-making under pressure.
- Implement a monitoring system that automatically alerts air traffic control and airline management if a plane's fuel level becomes critically low.
- Instruct crews to handle all in-flight issues internally to maintain the airline's public image.

Chapter 1

Voices Unheard: The Silent Impact of Psychological Safety

In Chapter Zero, we examined dramatic and tragic real-world scenarios that demonstrated the dire consequences of lacking psychological safety. These extreme instances shed light on the often-overlooked power of psychological safety in our work environments.

However, what happens on a day-to-day basis in organizations when psychological safety is absent? How does it subtly yet significantly impact team dynamics, workforce creativity, and overall company health?

This chapter delves into the less dramatic but equally impactful world of everyday work life. We explore the silent yet profound effect that psychological safety, or its absence, has on innovation, employee engagement, and organizational resilience.

Through the stories of individuals in various professional settings, we uncover how psychological safety can be an unseen force that either drives a company toward success or subtly undermines its foundations.

From high school students on an excursion to software engineers working on high-stakes projects, let's explore the untold stories of 'Voices Unheard' and understand why psychological safety is not only about preventing catastrophes but also about nurturing an environment where every voice can contribute to collective success.

Real-Life Scenarios:

High School Excursion (Meena's Dilemma):

Context: Meena, a knowledgeable student on a school trip, notices potential danger on a forest trail.

Challenge: She chooses silence over speaking up about the risks due to the fear of being mocked or dismissed by her peers.

Impact: Her decision potentially places the entire group in harm's way, highlighting how a lack of psychological safety can have real-world consequences.

Software Consultancy Firm (Ravi's Hesitation):

Context: Ravi, a new engineer, faces challenges with a project timeline but hesitates to communicate his concerns.

Challenge: His fear of appearing incompetent or slow prevents him from seeking help or suggesting timeline adjustments.

Impact: The project suffers delays, causing stress within the team and reducing overall productivity.

Tech Start-Up (Rajesh's Innovation):

Context: Rajesh has an innovative idea for his company's product but is reluctant to share it.

Challenge: He fears his idea might be rejected or ridiculed by a manager who prefers sticking to the routine.

Impact: The company misses out on a potentially groundbreaking feature, which a competitor later capitalizes on.

COST OF FEAR

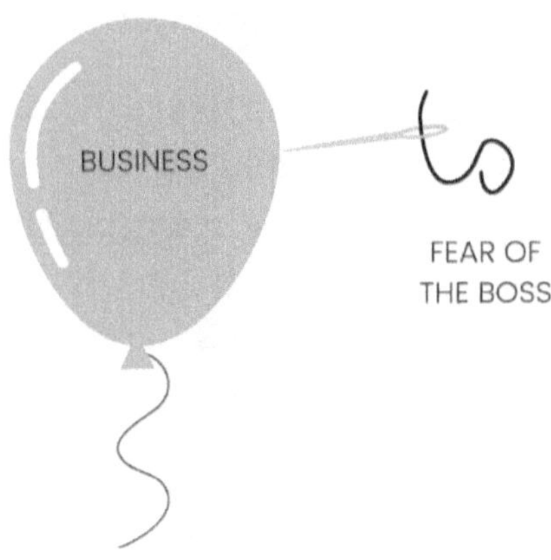

Data Science Project (AI Model Flaw):

Context: An experienced data scientist discovers a flaw in an AI model but fears the repercussions of speaking up.

Challenge: Concerned about disrespecting senior colleagues, the individual remains silent.

Impact: The unaddressed flaw could lead to a flawed product release, affecting customer satisfaction and the company's reputation.

Preschool Painting (Aarav's Choice):

Context: Young Aarav, in preschool, faces a choice between following his preference or conforming to peer pressure.

Challenge: His previous experience of being teased leads him to suppress his individuality.

Impact: Aarav's creative expression is stifled, illustrating the importance of psychological safety even in early childhood.

The individuals involved in these situations were unable to express their thoughts, fears, or ideas. It wasn't because they lacked the skills or knowledge but rather because they felt unsafe to do so. They feared judgment, ridicule, or professional backlash, and these fears prevented them from speaking up, even when lives were at risk.

Now, let's apply this concept to your own experiences in your workplaces and organizations. You may be thinking that the consequences of lacking psychological safety in your team or organization aren't as immediate or severe as a plane crash or spacecraft disintegration. And you're right; the impacts are often not as immediate or dramatic.

However, the underlying dynamics are the same. When individuals don't feel safe to voice their concerns, ask questions, or present new ideas, it can have significant long-term impacts on the organization.

These impacts can include reduced innovation, lower productivity, decreased employee engagement, and, ultimately, a decreased ability to compete in the market.

In your role, you may encounter a situation where you have an idea that could potentially improve a project or identify a potential flaw in a project plan. If you feel unsafe to share your concerns or ideas, the project may proceed without the benefit of your insight, leading to sub-optimal outcomes. Although the consequences may not be immediate, they can still have a significant impact on the organization's success.

Similarly, when considering your personal growth within an organization, imagine a situation where you feel unsafe asking questions or seeking help due to a fear of appearing incompetent. This fear can hinder your learning and growth, resulting in long-term consequences for your career.

Remember the scenario involving Aarav in the preschool? While the stakes may seem lower, the principle remains the same. If a child feels unsafe to express their individuality, it can inhibit their creativity and personal growth. Psychological safety, or the lack thereof, affects all aspects of life—it's just the scale of the impact and the time it takes to become apparent that varies.

The Heart of Psychological Safety:

At its core, psychological safety is about creating an environment where every voice matters. It's about ensuring that open, honest communication is not just welcomed but encouraged, fostering a culture where innovation and growth can flourish.

In the Upcoming Chapters:

We will explore the concept of psychological safety in-depth, understanding its importance, how it compounds over time, and how we can improve it in the workplace.

ACTIVITIES:

As a manager, what action would you take to encourage team members, especially newer ones, to speak up about project concerns?

- Hold regular one-on-one meetings to build trust and open communication.
- Create an anonymous feedback system for sharing concerns.
- Publicly recognize and reward team members who raise valid concerns.
- State explicitly that all opinions are valued during team meetings.
- Remind team members that failing to meet deadlines could result in negative performance reviews.

As a teacher overseeing a school trip, would you implement a specific protocol that encourages students to report any safety concerns without fear of ridicule?

- Yes
- No

The Power of Compounding: Lessons from Chinese Bamboo and Companies Like Flipkart & Infosys

Imagine tending to a Chinese bamboo tree in your garden, a unique plant that takes five years to show any visible growth. For the first four years, there is no activity above ground, but in the fifth year, the tree suddenly sprouts and grows to an astonishing height of 80 feet in just six weeks.

This growth pattern, although peculiar, serves as a metaphor for the principle of compounding. It applies not only to bamboo trees but also to our investments, behaviors, and even organizational cultures.

Indian companies like Flipkart and Infosys exemplify the power of compounding. Through initial investments and exponential growth, ordinary employees became millionaires, experiencing life-changing outcomes. These success stories illustrate the positive impact of compounding. However, it is essential to recognize that compounding can also intensify downfall.

To illustrate this point, let's examine the story of General Electric (GE). Under the leadership of Jack Welch, GE's market value skyrocketed from $12 billion to $410 billion. Welch's relentless pursuit of short-term profits and market leadership fostered an aggressive culture where internal competition thrived and open communication was stifled. This approach led to significant growth and earned Welch the title of "Manager of the Century" by Fortune in 1999.

Unfortunately, the aggressive culture at GE had been silently festering beneath the surface, much like the hidden growth of a bamboo tree. When Jeff Immelt took over as CEO after Welch's retirement, these underlying issues began to emerge.

Immelt, who faced criticism for his leadership style, had to confront the compounded effects of years of internal competition, lack of open communication, and a short-term focus. Sustaining the company's growth became increasingly challenging.

The fear-driven culture at GE stifled innovation and suppressed voices, gradually taking a toll on the company. GE faced significant setbacks, including writing off billions due to poor acquisitions, insurance liabilities, and a struggling power business. In 2018, after over a century, GE was removed from the Dow Jones Industrial Average, and its share price plummeted, erasing over $200 billion in market value.

The Shocking Revelation

This story reveals that compounding, often associated with financial growth, can also amplify organizational failures. Welch's intense focus on short-term gains had long-lasting effects on GE, impacting the company even after his departure and setting the stage for Immelt's challenging tenure. It underscores the importance of fostering a psychologically safe culture that encourages open communication and long-term thinking, which are crucial for sustainable growth.

Building such a culture may not yield immediate and visible results, much like nurturing a Chinese bamboo tree. However, over time, it can lead to significant, positive transformation. Conversely, neglecting to foster such a culture can have catastrophic consequences, as seen in the case of General Electric.

As we navigate our personal and professional lives, we are planting seeds. The question we must ask ourselves is whether we are preparing for exponential growth or unknowingly setting the stage for our own downfall.

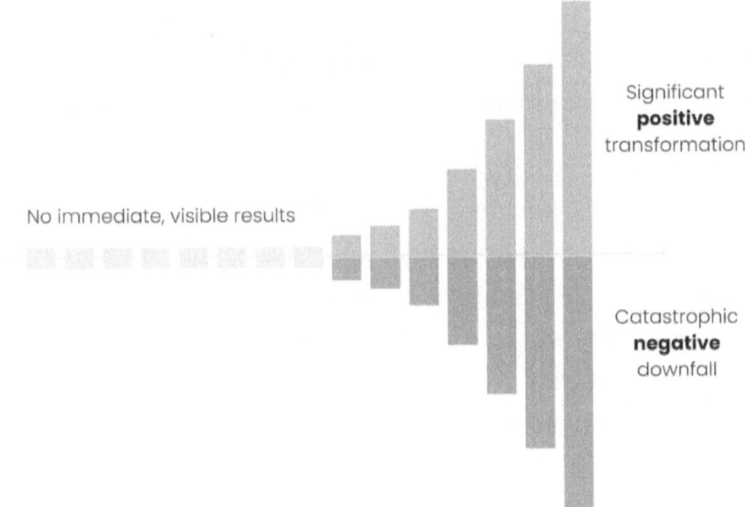

Takeaways

Power of Compounding:

The principle of compounding impacts not only investments but also organizational culture and individual behavior.

Role of Leadership:

Leadership styles and organizational cultures can compound over time, either paving the way for future success or sowing the seeds of decline.

Silent Growth or Decline:

Similar to the Chinese bamboo tree, the effects of compounding may not be immediately visible but can suddenly appear in surprising ways.

Two Faces of Compounding:

Compounding can result in exponential growth, as demonstrated by companies like Flipkart and Infosys. However, it can also amplify mistakes and problems, leading to significant downfalls, as evidenced by the case of General Electric.

ACTIVITIES:

As a manager, you're tasked with driving rapid growth at your company. Which approach would you choose to motivate your team?

- Implement aggressive growth targets and competitive incentives, putting pressure on teams to deliver quick results even if it risks creating a high-stress environment.
- Encourage a culture of innovation and patience, rewarding long-term success and sustainable practices over immediate achievements.
- Focus on developing individual employee skills and fostering leadership at all levels to ensure growth is both shared and sustainable.
- Maintain current operational strategies but increase marketing efforts to boost growth without altering internal culture significantly.

You've discovered a significant flaw in your company's main product line. How would you address this issue?

- Keep the issue under wraps while a solution is sought to avoid panic and protect the company's stock price.
- Immediately inform all stakeholders and initiate a transparent process to solve the issue, ensuring all teams are involved in the solution.
- Launch an internal investigation to determine responsibility before taking any external actions.
- Assess the financial impact of potential fixes versus the cost of a recall, choosing the most economical option.

Chapter 3

The Impact of Compounding in Psychological Safety

In our exploration of the powerful yet subtle force of compounding in the workplace, let's revisit Ravi's story from the previous chapter. Ravi, a new software engineer, entered his career with enthusiasm and innovative ideas.

However, his initial experiences in the workplace reflect a common reality for many of us.

Ravi's Initial Enthusiasm:

Fresh and eager, Ravi embarked on his new role with a wealth of ideas and a strong desire to contribute. His fresh perspective held the potential to bring innovative solutions and improvements to his team.

Initial Dismissal and Its Effect:

Unfortunately, Ravi's excitement was short-lived. His ideas and contributions were repeatedly overlooked or dismissed by his manager. While not overtly hostile, this dismissal was enough to make Ravi doubt the value of his input.

The Erosion of Ravi's Enthusiasm:

As time went on, Ravi became more withdrawn. His once vibrant stream of ideas began to dry up as he started holding back, avoiding the discomfort of being continually disregarded.

The Compounding Loss:

Ravi's story highlights a significant and often underestimated aspect of psychological safety - its compounding effect. Despite the team still functioning, they were now operating without the full potential of Ravi's contributions. Initially seemingly insignificant, this loss compounded over time, resulting in a significant deficit in creativity and innovation within the team.

Reflecting on the Long-Term Impact:

The true cost of the lack of psychological safety in Ravi's case, similar to the growth of the Chinese bamboo tree, was not immediately visible. It is a subtle and slow process, where the full impact of lost opportunities and diminished engagement becomes apparent over time. By the time the manager who did not understand Ravi has moved to a different company, the consequences would have become evident.

Takeaways:

The Subtle Erosion:

The absence of psychological safety may not immediately disrupt team function, but it gradually erodes potential and growth over time.

Lost Opportunities for Innovation:

Employees like Ravi, when they do not feel heard or valued, tend to withdraw their ideas, resulting in a cumulative loss of innovation and growth potential for the organization.

The Long Game of Culture Building:

Building a psychologically safe workplace is akin to nurturing a Chinese bamboo tree — it requires a long-term investment. Its true value and impact unfold gradually but are substantial.

ACTIVITIES

You notice a team member like Ravi becoming less engaged and withdrawn over time after their ideas are dismissed. How would you respond to this situation as a manager?

- Do nothing and assume Ravi will adjust and eventually find his place in the team.
- Schedule a one-on-one meeting with Ravi to openly discuss his feelings and reassure him that his ideas are valued.
- Provide formal feedback on Ravi's suggestions, explaining why they were dismissed and encouraging him to continue contributing.
- Implement a team-wide initiative that encourages more open and supportive communication and recognizes contributions from all team members.

As a Manager, how would you address the broader issue of overlooked contributions within your team to prevent the compounding loss of innovation?

- Continue with the current management style, prioritizing efficiency, and established ideas over new suggestions.
- Introduce a new policy where all team members can submit ideas anonymously to be reviewed and discussed in monthly meetings.
- Organize regular brainstorming sessions that allow every team member, regardless of seniority, to pitch ideas directly to leadership.
- Conduct training sessions for managers on the importance of psychological safety and how to cultivate it within their teams.

Chapter 4

The Misunderstood Paradox – Thriving in Spite of Fear

I see the question forming on your lips, the doubt creeping into your mind. "If lack of psychological safety is so detrimental," you ask, "why do so many companies that treat their employees poorly continue to survive and even thrive?"

That's a valid question, and to answer it, we need to venture beyond superficial appearances. Yes, organizations can and do achieve short-term success despite poor employee management and a lack of psychological safety. They might do so by leveraging aggressive sales strategies, dominant market positions, or sheer financial muscle. But as Elon Musk wisely said, "Great companies are built on great products." In the long term, companies that neglect their employees' well-being risk losing their ability to innovate and adapt – key elements for sustained success in today's rapidly evolving world.

Many companies equate survival with success, a misunderstanding that obscures the long-term realities. Profitability and longevity are parts of the success equation, but they are not the only variables. What about employee satisfaction, innovation, adaptability, and societal impact? A company might stay afloat and turn profits, but is it truly succeeding if it can't inspire and foster a harmonious and creative work environment?

One could argue that numerous companies have withstood the test of time, standing tall for over a century. Indeed, longevity is a form of success, but it's worth pondering whether they've reached their full potential. Imagine a world where these century-old companies fostered an environment of psychological safety. How much more innovation, growth, and positive societal impact might they have achieved?

The truth is that a lack of psychological safety might not cause immediate failure, but it creates a subtle erosion, gradually undermining the organization's foundations over time. It's like termites gnawing away at a wooden structure, hardly noticeable until the edifice weakens and collapses. The absence of psychological safety creates an environment of fear and stifles innovation, preventing the company from reaching its potential. Moreover, without psychological safety, companies are one grave mistake away from a crisis that could wipe out their fortunes.

Survival in business is not merely about avoiding failure; it's about reaching your potential, and that's where psychological safety becomes paramount. It enables companies to foster innovation, nurture talent, and create sustainable success. The necessity of psychological safety becomes more evident when we shift our focus from surviving to truly thriving.

Let's delve deeper into understanding this crucial component that differentiates good companies from truly great ones. Psychological safety isn't just about preventing failure; it's about empowering success. As we explore further in our upcoming chapters, we'll see how companies that prioritize psychological safety not only survive but lead the way forward.

Takeaways

Survival vs. Thriving: Companies may survive without psychological safety, but they miss out on the full spectrum of success, including innovation, adaptability, and positive societal impact.

Erosion Over Time: Lack of psychological safety may not show immediate catastrophic effects but contributes to a gradual erosion of the company's foundational strength.

A Crisis Away: In an environment devoid of psychological safety, companies are always one significant mistake away from a situation that could cause irreparable damage.

ACTIVITIES

Your company is hit by a crisis due to a major oversight, which could have been prevented with better internal communication. As a leader, how would you reform the company culture to prevent such issues in the future?

- Focus on damage control and public relations to manage the crisis's impact without altering internal communication strategies.
- Implement comprehensive training on risk management and communication for all employees to ensure greater transparency and proactive issue reporting.
- Establish a transparent feedback mechanism where employees can report potential risks without fear of reprisal.
- Create a task force dedicated to analyzing and improving company policies related to risk and safety.

You're a leader at a company that has historically prioritized short-term profits over employee well-being. After learning about the importance of psychological safety, how would you begin to shift the company's focus toward more sustainable practices?

- Maintain the status quo to avoid disrupting current profit streams, even if it might harm long-term sustainability.
- Gradually integrate employee well-being initiatives into the business strategy, balancing profit goals with long-term health.

- Overhaul company policies immediately to prioritize psychological safety, potentially risking short-term profitability for long-term gains.
- Initiate a series of workshops and training sessions to educate management on the benefits of psychological safety for long-term success.

Chapter 5

Intangible But Indispensable

The Invisibility Cloak of Impact - From Intangible to Indispensable

As we navigate the business and social landscapes, psychological safety, much like air or gravity, remains a largely unnoticed and unacknowledged presence. Its impact is felt more in its absence than in its existence, largely because it is intangible and difficult to quantify. However, just like air and gravity, without it, our systems, our interactions, and our very existence would crumble.

Consider this: in the late 19th century, the field of public health was revolutionized by the germ theory of disease. Until then, medical professionals believed in the 'miasma theory', the idea that diseases were caused by 'bad air.' The notion that microscopic organisms could cause illness was initially ridiculed, primarily because germs couldn't be seen.

However, once accepted and understood, the germ theory brought about significant improvements in public health, leading to practices like sterilization and the development of antibiotics. Today, we take germ theory for granted, even though germs are invisible to the naked eye.

Now, let's draw a parallel with the corporate world. The business landscape is littered with the ruins of once-thriving companies that ignored the importance of psychological safety. Consider the case of Nokia, once a dominant player in the mobile phone industry. The company's fall from grace was attributed, in part, to a culture that didn't encourage open and honest communication. Employees were reportedly scared to voice their opinions or challenge decisions, leading to an echo chamber that stifled innovation.

On the other hand, companies that have fostered psychological safety have reaped the benefits, even if they haven't explicitly recognized its role. Toyota, a key player in the automobile industry, is a prime example.

Their 'Andon Cord' system allowed any employee on the assembly line to stop production if they noticed a problem. This system created a culture where employees felt safe to voice concerns without fear of retribution, leading to high-quality products and efficient production. Yet, many wouldn't attribute Toyota's success to the concept of psychological safety.

A profound instance of an intangible construct that became indispensable, albeit non-physical, is the concept of 'credit'. Credit, a mere belief in someone's ability and commitment to repay borrowed money, transformed the world economy. Initially, it was just an abstract agreement between two parties. But as systems were established around it – like banking, credit ratings, and legislation – it became the bedrock of our economic structure. Today, it's a pivotal part of our lives; it's invisible but omnipresent and critical to our economic survival.

Similar to germs and credit, psychological safety is an intangible factor whose presence isn't physically felt but profoundly impacts the efficiency, productivity, and overall health of an organization. Its invisibility does not diminish its significance. The journey of acceptance for psychological safety, much like germs or credit, might be long, but as history shows us, it's often the unseen forces that shape our world most profoundly.

As we proceed to the next chapters, we will look at how we can foster psychological safety and the significant difference it can make in any work environment.

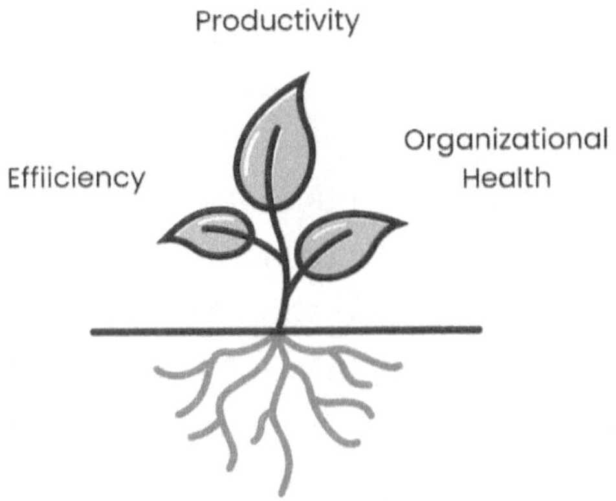

Takeaways

Psychological safety, although intangible, plays a critical role in organizational success.

The acceptance of intangible but crucial factors like psychological safety may take time, much like scientific theories or economic concepts, but they are nonetheless vital.

Just because something is invisible doesn't mean it's not impactful; in fact, it can be indispensable.

ACTIVITIES

You're at a company training session discussing the impacts of intangible factors like psychological safety on business success. How would you convince a skeptical manager of its importance?

- Dismiss their skepticism and continue with the established training program, assuming they'll eventually understand its importance.
- Use historical analogies, like the germ theory of disease, to illustrate how unseen factors can have critical impacts on outcomes.
- Provide empirical evidence from successful companies that have implemented psychological safety measures.
- Invite them to a workshop where they can see firsthand accounts and testimonies from employees in companies where psychological safety has made a measurable difference.

Your organization has a history of ignoring psychological safety, leading to high attrition and low innovation. As a new leader, what initiative would you prioritize to start changing this culture?

- Continue with the current culture while focusing on increasing profit margins and market share, assuming that success can compensate for the lack of psychological safety
- Implement an open-door policy and regular town hall meetings to encourage open communication and feedback.
- Develop a comprehensive onboarding process that emphasizes the value of psychological safety and its expectations for all employees.
- Launch an individual team-wide recurring psychological safety session program that repeatedly insists on the importance of psychological safety and a regular check on how good team members feel about the initiative

Chapter 6

The Hidden Foundation

Let's meet Anita, a charismatic software engineer. Growing up in a humble home in Chennai, Anita was the youngest of three children. Her parents, both educators, instilled in their children the importance of open communication, respect, and mutual trust – the seeds of psychological safety.

They allowed their children to express their thoughts, ask questions, make mistakes, and learn from them. They nurtured an environment where their kids could thrive, each in their own unique way. As a student, Anita carried these values into her school and university life, where she excelled both academically and socially.

However, Anita didn't consciously attribute her success to the culture of psychological safety in which she was fortunate to grow up. She was always curious, a good listener, and a collaborative team player. But she never quite understood why she excelled in team projects and why her peers often turned to her for advice or help.

Upon graduation, Anita got her dream job at a well-respected multinational tech firm. Excited, she jumped headfirst into the corporate world. However, she soon noticed a stark difference between her personal life and professional life. The workplace did not reflect the safety and openness she was used to, and she found herself holding back on ideas and suggestions, something she had never experienced before.

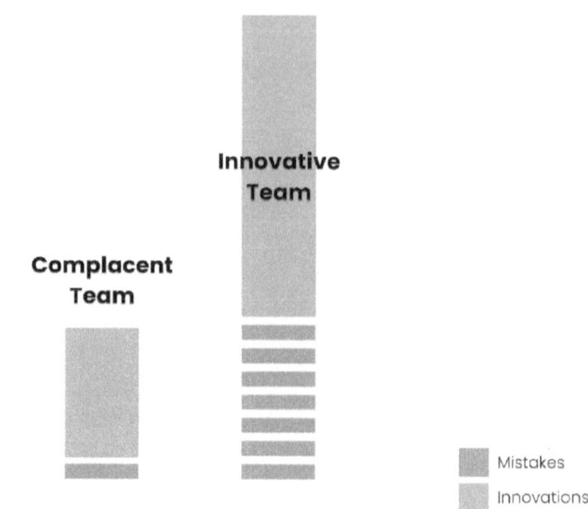

Better teams makes more mistakes;
And they become innovative.

An incident stands out in her memory. Anita noticed a critical bug in the code for a new software release, but her immediate manager, known for his volatile temper, had declared the code perfect and ready for launch.

Remembering a previous team meeting where a colleague was berated for pointing out an issue, Anita chose to stay silent. The software was released, and as feared, customers reported failures, and the company had to invest in significant damage control.

In another instance, Anita had an innovative idea for streamlining the software testing process. However, as a new team member, she hasn't felt comfortable sharing her ideas yet. She noticed that only the views of the senior team members were taken seriously, and others were expected to follow instructions without question.

So, Anita decided to hold onto her suggestion. The project went on for months, running into several delays due to inefficient testing methods.

Despite these experiences, Anita continued to excel in her personal life. Her friends and family often leaned on her for advice and support, and she was a sounding board for their ideas and worries.

It was during one of these discussions with her old school friend, Arun, a human resources professional, that she first heard about the term "psychological safety". As Arun described the concept, Anita was able to connect the dots – she realized what she had been taking for granted all her life and what was starkly missing from her professional environment.

We can relate to individuals like Anita, who possess talent and skills that can greatly benefit organizations yet are not fully utilized.

Takeaways

Psychological safety can be taken for granted by those who have grown up in environments where it is nurtured. It was deeply ingrained in Anita's upbringing and played a crucial role in her early academic and social successes. She was only able to understand its value when it was absent. Even individuals who do great work and are creative can lose all of it when they lack psychological safety.

Even talented and naturally collaborative individuals like Anita can struggle in professional settings that don't foster psychological safety.

Organizations can suffer concrete setbacks, such as software bugs or inefficient processes, due to a lack of psychological safety.

ACTIVITIES

You notice that a team member, similar to Anita, seems hesitant to share their thoughts during meetings. What approach would you take to encourage them?

- Ignore their hesitation, assuming they will speak up when they feel it's necessary.

- After the meeting, approach them privately to ask about their thoughts and reassure them that their input is valued.
- Publicly encourage them during meetings to share their ideas, highlighting the importance of every team member's contributions.
- Implement a 'round robin' approach in meetings where each team member, including the quieter ones, is given time to speak without interruptions.

A situation arises where a bug similar to what Anita found has been overlooked and could potentially escalate. How would you address the team's handling of the issue?

- Publicly reprimand those responsible for missing the bug, emphasizing the importance of diligence.
- Review the incident privately with the team involved, focusing on what can be learned rather than assigning blame.
- Use the incident as a case study in the next team meeting to discuss lessons learned and how similar issues can be prevented.
- Update the project review protocols to include more rigorous checks, involving more team members in the process.

Chapter 7

The Hidden Power – An Unfamiliar Journey

Rohan, an ambitious product manager, grew up in a quaint town in Rajasthan, India, where traditions held strong. Respect for one's elders was paramount. From a young age, he was taught not to question the wisdom of his elders, who possessed knowledge passed down through generations. Rohan was expected to follow their guidance without dissent.

His academic excellence earned him a scholarship at one of India's top engineering colleges. However, the educational environment there mirrored the traditions of his hometown. Teachers were considered the ultimate authority, and students were expected to passively receive their teachings without engaging in debates.

Soon after, Rohan found employment at a leading global tech firm in Bangalore. Every day, he poured his heart into his work, striving for perfection in each task. However, something felt lacking.

Rohan's manager, Maya, was unlike anyone he had ever encountered. Maya had been mentored by a forward-thinking manager who believed in growth mindsets and valued the individuality of every team member.

Maya's leadership style reflected this philosophy. She actively sought opinions, encouraged discussions, and remained unfazed by disagreements. For Rohan, who had been conditioned to unquestioningly accept authority, this was unsettling.

During a team meeting, Rohan noticed a potential flaw in a product design. Part of him wanted to share his observation, but his ingrained deference to authority kept him silent. Weeks later, during testing, the flaw became apparent, causing a delay in the product launch and additional work for the team.

On another occasion, Rohan came up with an innovative feature that he believed would enhance user experience. However, haunted by past experiences and uncertain of how his idea would be received, he chose to remain silent. Ironically, a few months later, a competitor launched a strikingly similar feature, receiving praise and generating profits.

Amidst his internal conflicts, Rohan couldn't help but notice something extraordinary. Under Maya's leadership, his team thrived in ways others didn't. They were happier, more creative, and consistently delivered exceptional results. Rohan observed that his teammates were genuinely invested in their work, driven by passion rather than compulsion. This observation piqued Rohan's interest.

His understanding deepened during an in-house workshop on team dynamics, where the concept of "psychological safety" was introduced. As the facilitator delved into the topic, Rohan had a realization. Maya's management style wasn't just a quirk; it was a carefully thought-out strategy to cultivate an environment of trust and mutual respect.

Rohan's initial discomfort stemmed from his unfamiliarity with such a supportive workplace culture. He came to appreciate the value of an environment where everyone felt safe to express themselves, ultimately leading to increased innovation and efficiency.

For many of us, our past experiences may have conditioned us to withhold our ideas or opinions. And, like Rohan, we may later regret our silence, especially when someone else acts upon a similar idea with great success. This story highlights the transformative power of psychological safety in fostering innovation, collaboration, and overall team success.

ACTIVITIES

As Rohan begins to appreciate the supportive culture under Maya's leadership, how can he contribute to sustaining this environment?

- Maintain a passive role, enjoying the benefits of the environment without actively contributing to it.
- Offer to lead a workshop sharing his journey from hesitancy to active participation, encouraging others who might feel the same.
- Become an advocate for psychological safety in the workplace, promoting practices that support open communication and respect.
- Regularly provide positive feedback to peers and Maya, reinforcing the behaviors that foster a healthy team dynamic.

You are Maya and believe that team members, including Rohan, have unutilized potential. What initiative might you introduce to uncover and nurture this talent?

- Maintain current roles and responsibilities, focusing on efficiency rather than potential exploration.
- Organize a "hackathon" or innovation day where team members can work on projects outside their usual responsibilities.
- Implement a "talent showcase" where team members can present a skill or project related to or outside their regular duties.
- Create a mentorship program encouraging team members to explore new areas under the guidance of more experienced colleagues.

Chapter 8

A Cascade of Stress and the Imperative of Psychological Safety

The fast-paced nature of today's workplace often resembles high-stakes and high-pressure environments found in space exploration or healthcare. Although the immediate risks may not be as severe or life-threatening, the long-term consequences can be harmful to both individuals and organizations.

Additionally, the effects of stress, burnout, and poor decision-making can create a ripple effect, impacting employees, customers, and the wider community. In this context, psychological safety becomes a crucial foundation for sustainable success.

PSYCHOLOGICAL SAFETY IS NOT ONLY AN **ETHICAL RESPONSIBILITY** BUT ALSO A **STRATEGIC IMPERATIVE**.

Modern workplaces frequently demand high levels of productivity, which pushes employees to constantly perform at their best. In such environments, fear of failure and the pressure to succeed can cultivate a culture of stress and anxiety. This fear can discourage individuals from voicing concerns, admitting mistakes, or proposing innovative ideas, similar to incidents like the Mars Climate Orbiter mission or the Therac-25 incidents. This culture of fear stifles innovation, lowers morale, and ultimately affects the overall performance and product quality of the organization.

Furthermore, the effects of this stress extend beyond the workplace, impacting physical health, mental well-being, and relationships in employees' personal lives. These effects also trickle down to customers in the form of subpar products, poor service, and inconsistent delivery. Consequently, customers experience added stress, creating a destructive, intangible cycle that affects a broader population.

Psychological safety becomes paramount in breaking this cycle. When employees feel safe to express their thoughts, admit mistakes, and engage in healthy discussions, they are less likely to experience the detrimental effects of chronic stress. They become more invested in their work, perform better, and contribute positively to the organization's culture.

Moreover, the benefits of psychological safety extend to customers as well. When employees feel safe to innovate and challenge the status quo, it leads to the creation of superior products and services. Consistency and predictability improve, enhancing customer satisfaction and loyalty.

In essence, psychological safety acts as a defense against the cascade of stress in the modern workplace. By fostering a culture of openness and respect, organizations can mitigate the risks of burnout, cultivate a healthier work environment, and provide better services and products to their customers. Thus, psychological safety becomes not only an ethical responsibility but also a strategic imperative in today's complex and demanding workplace.

ACTIVITIES

Your team is under significant stress due to a critical product launch. A team member has an innovative but untested idea that could improve the product. How do you respond?

- Acknowledge it when they communicate it and later forget it.
- Create a safe space to explore the idea, possibly through a small-scale pilot or simulation, without derailing the main project timeline.
- Acknowledge the idea but decide to revisit it after the product launch to maintain focus.
- Encourage the team member to develop the idea further on their own time if they are passionate about its potential.

A mistake made by a team member is discovered, which could delay the project and impact client relations. How would you handle this situation to maintain psychological safety?

- Reprimand the team members publicly to set an example and prevent future mistakes.
- Address the mistake in a private meeting, discussing what went wrong and how similar issues can be prevented in the future.
- Use this as a learning opportunity for the whole team, emphasizing the value of learning from errors without singling out the individual responsible.
- Ignore the error to maintain morale and ask other team members to cover it up.

Chapter 9

Psychological Safety: A Panacea?

In today's rapidly evolving world, businesses constantly face increasing complexity and change. Organizations strive to create an environment that fosters learning, innovation, and performance. This is where the concept of

"Psychological Safety" comes into play, becoming something of a holy grail in the field of organizational development.

However, as with any concept gaining momentum, there is a risk of misinterpretation or oversimplification. Is psychological safety the ultimate solution to all organizational challenges? Let's explore.

Psychological safety allows for moderate risk-taking, speaking one's mind and creativity, and taking initiative without fear of negative consequences. Such behaviors lead to better collaboration and innovation, opening up avenues for communication and leveraging each team member's unique strengths, perspectives, and experiences.

Without psychological safety, individuals may hold back their expression, ideas, or mistakes, limiting the collective intelligence and capacity for innovation and adaptability within a team.

HOW CAN TEAMS ACHIEVE
THEIR FULL POTENTIAL

However, it would be incorrect to see psychological safety as a cure-all. A team can have psychological safety but still underperform if there are no clear goals, lack of direction, or low-performance standards. Ultimately, teams need a combination of psychological safety and high-performance standards to reach their full potential.

Psychological safety is not about avoiding conflict or being overly nice. On the contrary, it's about fostering an environment where conflicts and disagreements can be openly and respectfully discussed, leading to more robust solutions and decisions.

Finally, psychological safety does not absolve individuals of their accountability. It is not an excuse for complacency or lack of effort. Rather, it encourages individuals to take responsibility for their actions and decisions because they know their team will support them.

In conclusion, while psychological safety is immensely valuable, it is not a panacea. It is a powerful element within a complex and interconnected ecosystem that drives team performance and organizational health. Like any other component of this ecosystem, it needs to be nurtured and maintained to yield lasting benefits.

ACTIVITIES

You're leading a team that enjoys a high level of psychological safety. However, recent project reviews suggest that performance is lagging. How do you address this while maintaining psychological safety?

- Lower performance standards to reduce pressure on the team, focusing solely on maintaining a safe environment.
- Introduce clear, measurable performance goals and regular feedback sessions that encourage accountability while maintaining a supportive atmosphere.
- Ignore the performance issues, prioritizing the preservation of psychological safety at all costs.
- Conduct a team workshop to collaboratively identify barriers to performance and develop strategies that align with maintaining psychological safety.

Your team feels safe to express ideas, but you notice that most suggestions are not particularly innovative or are too safe. How do you encourage more groundbreaking ideas?

- Praise all ideas equally to avoid discouraging team members, regardless of their innovation level.
- Challenge the team by setting higher expectations for innovation, providing examples and training on creative thinking techniques.
- Implement a reward system that specifically recognizes and rewards innovation and risk-taking.
- Accept the status quo, appreciating the team's comfort in expressing any ideas at all.

Chapter 10

Mum Effect

In high-stakes environments such as space exploration or healthcare, even the smallest oversights can have catastrophic consequences. Maintaining vigilance and exercising caution is crucial, and psychological safety plays a critical yet often overlooked role in these contexts.

Throughout our lives, we face rejections and judgments that may make us hesitant to voice our concerns, especially when they seem minor or trivial. This hesitation is amplified in the workplace, particularly in high-stakes industries where errors can have severe consequences.

Two notable examples come to mind: the Mars Climate Orbiter mission and the Therac-25 radiation therapy machine incidents. Both cases involved potentially avoidable mishaps, where seemingly minor details led to disastrous outcomes. Psychological safety may have played a key role in preventing these mishaps.

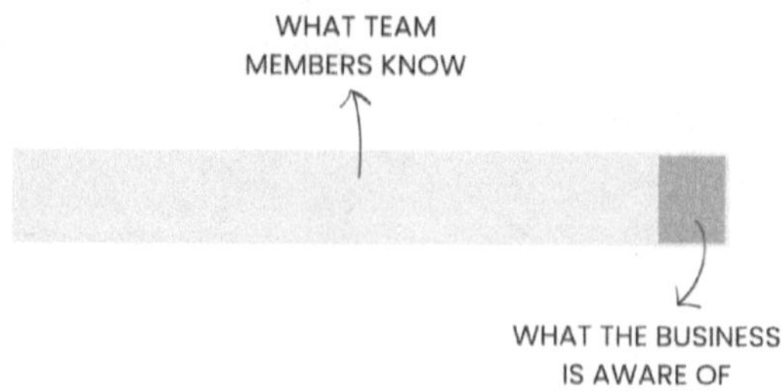

Team members know individually as time passes something is going to break. But the business is not aware of it.

The Mars Climate Orbiter was lost due to a simple unit conversion error. The Therac-25 accidents, on the other hand, were the result of small software bugs that led to patients receiving lethal doses of radiation. If someone had felt safe to speak up about their concerns or question the assumptions at play, these failures might have been prevented.

Then, there is the "Mum Effect", which refers to the human tendency to avoid communicating bad news or negative feedback. This effect is particularly pronounced in environments where psychological safety is lacking. Individuals might withhold pointing out problems or errors due to fear of retribution or blame.

However, in high-risk activities, it is precisely these minor concerns, these 'bad news' items, that need to be surfaced and addressed promptly. A culture that enables open communication, where errors, regardless of their scale, are shared without fear of judgment or punishment, can significantly reduce risks.

In healthcare or space exploration, professionals often deal with complex systems where minor details can have significant effects. Fostering a culture of psychological safety in such settings can help ensure that these details are not overlooked. Every team member, regardless of their role or position, should feel comfortable expressing their concerns or ideas.

In this light, we see that caution is not just about individual diligence. It is also about creating an environment where everyone feels safe to be cautious, question, clarify, and challenge. Such a culture of psychological safety is not a luxury—it is imperative for high-stakes, high-risk activities.

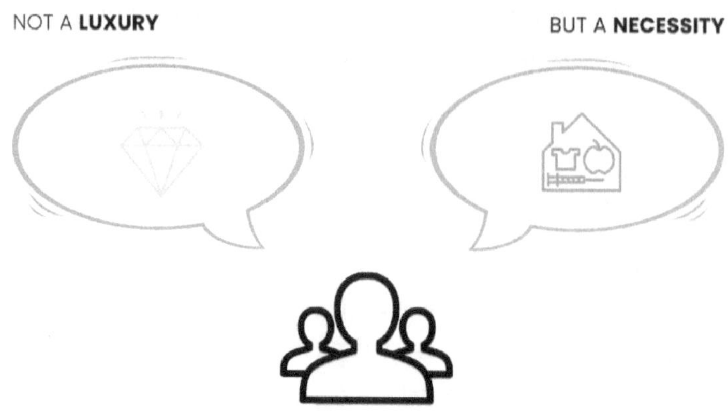

Psychological safety is not a **luxury**;
It's a **necessity** for thriving teams and innovative organizations.

In summary, while caution is of paramount importance in high-risk activities, it is often compromised by a lack of psychological safety. Only when individuals feel secure to communicate freely and voice their concerns can we maintain the necessary level of caution and prevent potential disasters. Building this environment is a critical task for any team or organization operating in high-risk domains. The stakes are simply too high to ignore the power of psychological safety.

ACTIVITIES

As a manager in a space agency, you've noticed some team members seem hesitant to report minor anomalies in test data. How would you encourage them to communicate these observations?

- Continue observing and document these hesitations without intervening, assuming they will resolve over time.
- Initiate a team meeting to emphasize the importance of reporting all data, regardless of perceived significance, and reassure them that all input is valuable.

- Implement an anonymous reporting system that allows team members to report their observations without fear of direct confrontation or blame.
- Reward team members who consistently report anomalies, even minor ones, to encourage a culture of vigilance.

You are a healthcare administrator, and a nurse reports a recurring minor issue with a piece of medical equipment that could become serious. What is your response to encourage a culture of safety?

- Thank the nurse for their vigilance but take no immediate action, assuming the issue is too minor to prioritize.
- Investigate the issue promptly, involving the nurse in the process to show that their concerns are taken seriously and acted upon.
- Set up a review committee to regularly discuss equipment feedback from staff, ensuring minor issues are addressed before they escalate.
- Document the feedback but focus on more pressing issues, citing resource constraints.

Chapter 11

A Gradual Transformation for Long-Term Growth

When a seed is sown, it does not become a towering tree overnight. It requires time, patience, nurturing, and most importantly, a belief in the natural process. The implementation of psychological safety within an organization or team is similar; it does not produce immediate, visible changes. The transformation is gradual, often unnoticed in the early stages, and becomes more apparent over time.

Understanding the timeline and trajectory of this change can be challenging, especially in fast-paced environments where immediate results are expected. However, numerous studies have demonstrated the long-term value and exponential benefits of psychological safety. For example, research from Google's Project Aristotle found that psychological safety was the most significant factor in building successful teams, leading to improved collaboration, innovation, and productivity.

Implementing psychological safety also requires a shift in mindset, particularly among leadership. Leaders are called upon to transition from traditional command-and-control management styles to a more empathetic and inclusive approach. This shift may be difficult, especially in cultures where empathy and vulnerability in the workplace are not the norm.

Nevertheless, this challenge is not insurmountable. Changing cultural norms and attitudes is indeed complex and requires sustained effort, but it is a journey worth taking. People on a path of self-discovery and self-growth may find it easier to make this shift. However, even those at the beginning of this journey can make significant progress with commitment, openness, and a willingness to learn.

Implementing psychological safety may be likened to steering a large ship—it does not turn on a dime, but with steady pressure and continual course corrections, it can change direction. With time, patience, and consistent effort, the benefits of a psychologically safe environment can and will be realized.

ACTIVITIES

As a leader accustomed to a command-and-control style, you're now aiming to foster psychological safety. How do you begin this transition in your management approach?

- Abruptly switch to a completely hands-off approach, assuming team members will immediately thrive with increased autonomy.
- Gradually introduce open communication forums, encouraging team members to share their thoughts and feedback in a structured manner.
- Provide training for yourself and other leaders on empathetic leadership and the principles of psychological safety.
- Delegate all decision-making to team members to promote empowerment without any guidance or boundaries.

You've implemented initiatives to increase psychological safety in your organization. How do you measure its impact over time, given that changes may not be immediately visible?

- Expect immediate improvements in team performance metrics and conclude the effort failed if no changes are seen within a few months.
- Use regular employee satisfaction surveys and feedback to gauge subtle changes in team dynamics and communication.
- Wait for annual review cycles to evaluate changes, assuming any significant developments will be obvious by then.
- Implement a continuous feedback mechanism that tracks small day-to-day improvements in team interactions and morale.

Chapter 12

The Case for Psychological Safety: Is it Really Worth it?

Countless companies across India have achieved growth and profitability without explicitly focusing on psychological safety. Naturally, the question arises: if success is possible without it, why should we invest our efforts in building psychological safety?

To answer this question, we need to reconsider our understanding of 'success.' While financial profitability is crucial, it is not the sole measure of success. The well-being of employees who form the foundation of these organizations, should also be considered. Their engagement, job satisfaction, and personal growth are essential aspects of sustainable long-term success. Furthermore, humans are bound to make mistakes.

Let me ask executives directly:

Would you fly in an airplane where the pilot is stressed out, knowing that humans, even well-trained ones, can make errors?

Consider the recent incident with a major food delivery service in India. A minor billing error, caused perhaps by a single overlooked bug in their software, led to a significant public relations crisis when customers accused the company of intentionally overcharging on social media. The issue went viral, causing reputational damage and requiring immediate action to correct the error and restore customer trust.

The key takeaway here is that for knowledge workers, the impact of their work, whether positive or negative, occurs at scale. Positive contributions often go unnoticed, but a single mistake can gain immediate attention and escalate into a crisis.

When we weigh the pros and cons of investing in a culture of psychological safety, consider this: a psychologically secure environment is not just an ethical necessity; it is practical. It allows for the early identification and rectification of errors before they escalate into larger issues that can harm your brand and bottom line.

India is currently facing a profound mental health crisis. According to WHO estimates (https://www2.deloitte.com/content/dam/Deloitte/global/Documents/Life-Sciences-Health-Care/gx-mental-health-2022-report-noexp.pdf), India's economic loss due to mental health conditions from 2012 to 2030 may reach a staggering $1.03 trillion. This figure highlights the fact that out of the 200 million people in India grappling with various mental health conditions, fewer than 30 million are seeking active care.

Creating psychologically safe environments in workplaces can significantly help prevent work-related stress and mental health issues, thereby mitigating this overwhelming socio-economic burden.

Psychological safety refers to an environment where employees feel secure in voicing ideas, expressing concerns, admitting mistakes, and taking risks without fear of criticism or punishment. Such an environment benefits not only individual employees but also the organization as a whole.

Here's how psychological safety can be a valuable asset:

Early Detection: If employees feel safe expressing their struggles, potential mental health issues can be detected early, leading to prompt intervention.

Better Treatment Adherence: Trust and open communication, byproducts of psychological safety, can improve adherence to treatments. Employees are less likely to discontinue their treatment due to fear of stigma or misunderstanding.

Prevention: Psychologically safe environments can reduce the incidence of work-related mental health conditions by reducing stress, fostering a sense of belonging, and enhancing overall job satisfaction.

Building psychological safety in the workplace is not an easy task. It requires a shift in deep-seated organizational cultures and attitudes. However, as the mental health crisis escalates, the urgency for proactive prevention grows. By investing in psychological safety, businesses can play a pivotal role in curtailing this trend while simultaneously boosting productivity and performance.

Creating a mentally healthy society extends beyond the healthcare sector. All sectors, particularly businesses, need to actively participate in cultivating environments that prioritize mental health. After all, a healthy mind is a prerequisite for a thriving business and a prosperous nation.

Takeaways

Short-term growth without psychological safety is feasible. However, for organizations aiming for resilience, innovation, and sustainable long-term success, psychological safety is not an optional luxury—it is a fundamental necessity.

ACTIVITIES

As a leader, you notice increasing stress levels among your team, potentially leading to burnout and reduced productivity. How would you incorporate psychological safety to address these issues?

- Ignore the stress as a normal part of the job and focus on meeting business targets.
- Introduce stress management workshops and encourage open discussions about workload and pressure.
- Implement a policy where employees can anonymously submit concerns about their work environment, which are then addressed in a monthly meeting.
- Regularly schedule one-on-one meetings with team members to discuss their well-being and any professional concerns they might have

A software bug in your company leads to a public relations issue. What steps would you take to ensure such errors are caught earlier, considering the need for psychological safety?

- Punish the team responsible for the bug to set an example for other employees.
- Review the incident openly with the team, focusing on learning from the mistake and preventing future occurrences.
- Implement a strict review process for all future software releases, adding pressure to the development team.
- Encourage a culture where employees feel safe to report potential bugs or errors without fear of blame or retribution.

Chapter 13

Five Stages of Team Development

Psychological safety significantly impacts the stages of team development, fostering effective collaboration and communication. These stages, introduced by psychologist Bruce Tuckman (https://www.wcupa.edu/coral/tuckmanStagesGroupDelvelopment.aspx), are forming, storming, norming, performing, and adjourning (https://www.wcupa.edu/coral/tuckmanStagesGroupDelvelopment.aspx). Let's explore each stage and understand how psychological safety influences them.

1. Forming:

During this stage, team members are polite and reserved as they get to know each other.

With Psychological Safety: Openness to a diversity of thought accelerates the process of getting to know one another.

Without Psychological Safety, Fear of rejection or ridicule may cause people to stick to polite conversations and withhold innovative ideas or concerns.

2. Storming:

Conflict and disagreement arise as individual differences surface.

With Psychological Safety: Conflict is viewed as a source of creative tension and a platform for exploring different viewpoints, leading to more innovative solutions.

Without Psychological Safety, Conflict can lead to defensiveness, blame games, and a non-cooperative environment, hindering progress.

3. Norming:

Team members start to resolve their differences, appreciate colleagues' strengths, and recognize common goals.

With Psychological Safety: The team actively seeks and gives feedback. Trust allows team members to admit weaknesses and mistakes, fostering a culture of learning and growth.

Without Psychological Safety, Superficial agreement may occur, leading to passive aggression and hiding of weaknesses and mistakes, potentially causing failures.

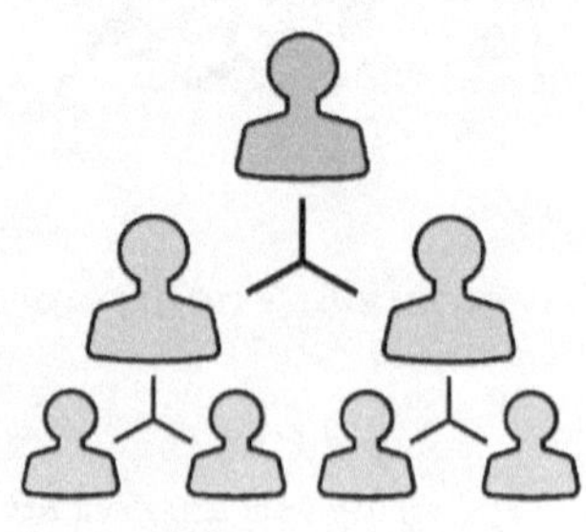

Psychological safety can ensure this information easily passed up the hierarchy and value can be protected

4. Performing:

The team effectively and efficiently delivers toward the common goal.

With Psychological Safety: The team is highly collaborative, innovative, and flexible. They communicate openly and constructively and challenge each other.

Without Psychological Safety, Success may be achieved, but it is likely despite the team dynamics. Information is often hoarded, inhibiting the team's full potential.

5. Adjourning (or Mourning):

The team project comes to an end, and team members part ways.

With Psychological Safety: The team celebrates achievements together and reflects on failures and learnings, strengthening their ability for future collaborations.

Without Psychological Safety, Blame games and negative sentiments may arise, causing a lack of closure and potential distrust in future collaborations.

Impact on a New Team Member

The presence or absence of psychological safety significantly influences the integration of a new team member.

With Psychological Safety: The new member is welcomed, their ideas are valued, and they are encouraged to take intellectual risks, accelerating their integration into the team.

Without Psychological Safety, The new member may feel isolated, undervalued, and anxious about expressing their ideas, slowing down their integration and reducing their effectiveness.

In conclusion, psychological safety enhances each stage of team development and facilitates smooth transitions. It reduces conflict, miscommunication, and mistrust, enabling teams to work more efficiently and effectively toward their common goal.

ACTIVITIES

You're leading a newly formed team with diverse backgrounds. How do you foster psychological safety to enhance team cohesion from the start?

- Encourage team members to keep their interactions formal and task-focused to avoid potential conflicts.
- Organize informal get-togethers and encourage the sharing of personal and professional backgrounds to build mutual understanding.
- Implement a rule where only work-related discussions are allowed during meetings to maintain professionalism.
- Start meetings with a 'check-in' round where each member shares something about their week, fostering openness and personal connection.
- Do not say anything about how to communicate and let the team decide how to do it.

- Introduce a "vulnerability bonus" for team members who share personal challenges or mistakes related to work, showing that vulnerability is valued and rewarded within the team.

As your team moves into the norming stage, how would you foster an environment where feedback is actively sought and given?

- Wait for team members to start giving feedback on their own.
- Implement regular feedback sessions, teaching team members how to give constructive feedback and how to receive it gracefully.
- Discourage feedback on personal performance to avoid potential conflicts and focus on project metrics only.
- Recognize and reward team members who openly share their weaknesses and ask for feedback.

Chapter 14

Reducing Information Asymmetry and Blame Games

Information asymmetry within teams occurs when some members have access to critical information that others do not. This unequal distribution creates power imbalances, fosters mistrust, and hinders collaboration, ultimately undermining team performance. Blame games, on the other hand, are a symptom of a low-trust environment where team members deflect accountability and cast blame on others to avoid negative consequences.

Psychological Safety and Information Asymmetry:

A lack of psychological safety worsens information asymmetry. In an environment where team members fear criticism or punitive action, they might hoard information defensively. This behavior seeks to maintain control or guard against perceived threats.

However, psychological safety mitigates information asymmetry in several ways:

1. Promoting Open Communication: Team members freely share information when they feel safe, encouraging knowledge sharing and collaborative problem-solving.

2. Facilitating Active Listening: Psychological safety fosters active listening, where team members value each other's input and ideas.

3. Encouraging Inclusivity: In psychologically safe teams, everyone's voice matters. This ensures that crucial information isn't monopolized by a select few, countering power imbalances.

Psychological Safety and Blame Games:

Blame games thrive in low-trust environments characterized by fear and defensiveness. However, psychological safety helps curtail this destructive pattern.

1. Cultivating Accountability: In psychologically safe teams, individuals take responsibility for their actions. Instead of blaming others, they openly discuss mistakes as opportunities for learning and growth.

2. Building Trust: Trusting team members understand that everyone is working toward the same goal. They appreciate mutual support and collaboration, reducing the urge to cast blame.

3. Encouraging Constructive Feedback: Psychological safety enables team members to provide and receive feedback in a positive, constructive manner. Instead of blaming others for failures, they engage in productive discussions to identify areas of improvement.

In conclusion, psychological safety combats information asymmetry and blame games, fostering trust, transparency, and collaboration.

ACTIVITIES

You're leading a project where you notice that critical information tends to be held by a few senior team members, leaving others out of the loop. How would you use principles of psychological safety to address this issue?

- Maintain the status quo as it ensures that sensitive information is handled by experienced team members.

- Implement a knowledge-sharing platform where all project-related information is accessible to every team member, reinforcing transparency.
- Organize regular team meetings where everyone is encouraged to share updates and critical information, promoting a culture of open communication.
- Only allow senior team members to access and disseminate crucial information, relying on their judgment for sharing it.

Your team is working on a highly confidential project, and the selective sharing of information has started to create divisions. How would you build trust and ensure psychological safety under these conditions?

- Continue with selective information sharing, as the project's sensitive nature justifies the approach.
- Hold confidential briefings with the whole team, explaining why certain information is restricted and reaffirming trust in each team member's role.
- Allow team members access to all information, disregarding the confidentiality risks.
- Create clear guidelines on information access and explain the reasons behind them to all team members, ensuring transparency about the process.

Chapter 15

The Value Equation – A Hidden Multiplier at Play

This chapter explores the elements that contribute to the value of an individual or team. We simplify these elements into five factors: Skills, Goals, Standards, Direction, and Learnability. These factors are intertwined, and one cannot thrive without the others.

Imagine these elements as pillars of a building. A deficiency in any one of them risks the stability of the entire structure. However, having strong and sturdy pillars is insufficient if the foundation - Psychological Safety - is weak.

This brings us to the powerful undercurrent of our value equation - Psychological Safety. It acts as an amplifier, magnifying the potential of all other factors when present or inhibiting them profoundly when absent.

*Value = (Skills * Goals * Standards * Direction * Learnability) ^ Psychological Safety*

By using Psychological Safety as an exponent, we illustrate that it is not just another factor. It is the environment within which the other factors operate, defining the dynamics of the team or organization.

Psychological safety is considered a continuum in a team, not a binary existence. It's about the collective experience of safety, not just a few "good" employees feeling secure. For the multiplier effect to fully kick in and generate sustainable results, everyone on the team should feel psychologically safe.

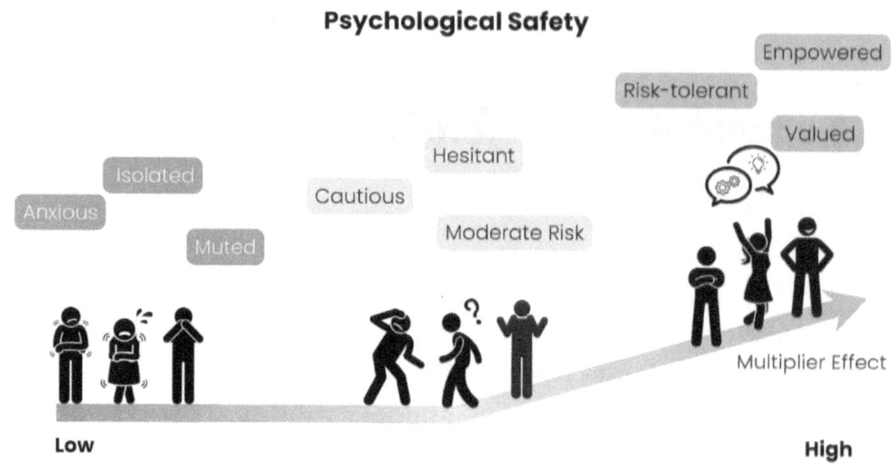

Remember, this formula is a simplified model that serves as a starting point for understanding the essential role Psychological Safety plays in team and organizational effectiveness. It underscores that Psychological Safety is not just a "nice to have"; it's a foundational element that amplifies the potential of all other factors.

ACTIVITIES

A team expresses a desire to learn new technologies to enhance their project outcomes but hesitates to take the first step. How would you use psychological safety to encourage their learnability?

- Mandate training sessions without addressing any underlying anxieties or resistance to change.
- Create a supportive learning environment where mistakes made during training are openly discussed and viewed as learning opportunities.

- Offer incentives for quickly mastering new skills, emphasizing speed and efficiency.
- Allow team members to choose their own learning paths and timelines to reduce pressure and enhance engagement.

Your team is eager to learn, but some members fear appearing incompetent by asking questions. How do you promote a learning environment where asking questions is seen as a strength, not a weakness?

- Criticize those who don't ask questions, assuming they are not interested in learning.
- Model the behavior by asking questions yourself and praising those who inquire or express curiosity.
- Implement a policy where only certain types of questions are allowed to prevent perceived incompetence.
- Conduct all trainings in a top-down lecture format to avoid any need for questions.

Chapter 16

Indications for a Business Owner/Manager to Find That There is Lack of Psychological Safety

Have you ever presided over a meeting where the entire room falls silent? Where participants merely nod in agreement, their faces devoid of enthusiasm or engagement, and no one challenges or questions what's being said?

There could be multiple reasons for an individual to remain silent, but when all the participants conform in this way, it often indicates a more pervasive issue. It's likely that there is a lack of psychological safety among the participants, either in your presence or due to other participants.

This silence, the absence of questions or ideas, is not merely a quirky team dynamic. It's a yellow flag in the short-term and a red flag in the long-term and a symptom of a pervasive issue. It likely indicates a lack of psychological safety among participants, either in your presence or due to others.

Psychological safety is not a luxury; it's a necessity for thriving teams and innovative organizations. When team members don't feel safe to speak up, disagree, or challenge the status quo, creativity is stifled, and opportunities are lost.

To detect this silent killer within your organization, watch out for these indications of a deficiency in psychological safety:

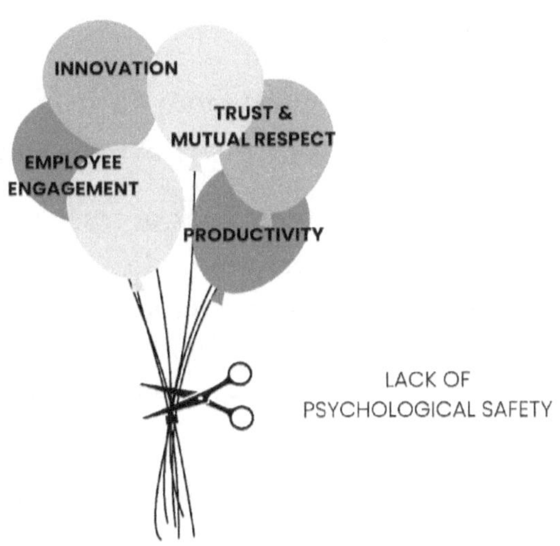

Tangible Indications

These are signs that can be readily observed and measured. They have a more immediate and noticeable impact on the organization.

1. **Silent Meetings:** No one speaks up, asks questions, or offers alternative perspectives.
2. **Stifled Communication:** Employees hold back ideas and concerns.
3. **Low Engagement:** Drop in participation and enthusiasm in team activities and projects.
4. **High Turnover Rates:** Regular resignations and a revolving door of new hires.
5. **Increased Conflict:** Petty disputes, misunderstandings, or open conflicts.

6. **Avoidance of Risk**: Over-cautious approach to tasks and projects.
7. **Customer Complaints**: Decrease in customer satisfaction due to lack of engagement and creativity.

Less Tangible Indications

These signs might be subtler and more difficult to pinpoint, yet they are deeply connected to the team's overall well-being and performance.

1. **Poor Peer Relationships**: Lack of trust among team members, leading to weak collaboration.
2. **Decline in Performance**: Subtle drop in performance levels and quality of work.
3. **Signs of Burnout**: Chronic stress and fatigue, sometimes leading to burnout.
4. **Lack of Personal Growth**: Stagnation in professional development.
5. **Resistance to Change**: Refusal to adapt to new initiatives or changes, reflecting underlying fears or insecurities.

Tangible and less tangible indications severely hamper an organization's ability to innovate, grow, and maintain a healthy culture. Recognizing these signs is the first step toward understanding and addressing the underlying issue of a lack of psychological safety.

These symptoms are not mere inconveniences but warning signs of a culture that does not foster trust, open dialogue, or personal growth. As a business owner or manager, recognizing these signs and taking proactive measures to cultivate psychological safety can turn around this stifling culture.

ACTIVITIES

In the software development team, you manage, feedback in PRs is often vague and non-specific, which you believe is due to a fear of offending colleagues. What would you do?

- Ignore the issue, assuming that feedback quality will improve on its own.
- Provide examples of constructive feedback during team meetings and highlight the benefits of specific, actionable comments.
- Require that all feedback must include specific suggestions for improvement.
- Conduct anonymous surveys to understand why team members are holding back and address identified concerns.

There's a noticeable increase in attrition among developers involved in the PR process. Exit interviews suggest that the review process feels overly critical and unsupportive.

- Dismiss the feedback as overly sensitive and continue with the current review process.
- Revise the review guidelines to emphasize support and constructive criticism and train reviewers on empathetic communication.
- Increase the frequency of reviews to boost familiarity and comfort among team members.
- Implement a mentoring system where more experienced developers provide one-on-one support to newer team members during their PRs.

You notice that several pull requests get approved without any comments or discussions. You suspect that team members might be hesitant to provide feedback.

- Continue to monitor the situation to see if it changes over time without intervention.
- Encourage more interactive review sessions by setting a minimum comment requirement for each PR.
- Organize a workshop to discuss the importance of feedback in PRs and establish norms that encourage constructive comments.
- Implement a rule where at least two approvals are required, with at least one comment or suggestion on each PR.

Chapter 17

Establishing Psychological safety

Establishing psychological safety in a team is essential for creating a healthy and productive work environment. As a business owner or manager, creating a space where employees feel safe to express their opinions, make mistakes, and learn from them is crucial. Here's how you can cultivate a psychologically safe environment.

Immediate Impact: Quick Wins for Psychological Safety

1. Lead by Example:

How to do this: As a leader, show vulnerability by openly admitting when you don't have all the answers. Ask for team input and genuinely consider their ideas. Appreciate and reward candid insights, and ensure there are systems in place to promote open dialogue.

Example: In a team meeting, say, "I'm unsure about the best approach for this project. What are your thoughts, team? I value your perspectives."

Impact: Builds trust and openness and encourages others to share their thoughts.

2. Encourage Open Communication:

How to do this: Regularly solicit feedback and show appreciation for differing opinions.

Example: Ask specific questions like, "Does anyone have different thoughts on this?" and positively acknowledge when someone shares an alternative view.

Impact: Fosters diversity of thought and empowers team members to speak up.

3. Establish Clear Boundaries:

How to do this: Clearly outline team roles, responsibilities, and acceptable behavior.

Example: Create a team charter that details everyone's roles and expected conduct, and have all team members agree to it.

Impact: Provides clear guidelines, reducing uncertainty and potential conflict

4. Address Issues Promptly:

How to do this: Act immediately on concerns or conflicts, showing that they are taken seriously.

Example: If a team member raises a concern about workload, schedule a meeting promptly to discuss and resolve the issue.

Impact: Shows responsiveness and care and builds trust in the organization.

5. Provide Safe Avenues for Feedback:

How to do this: Create anonymous channels for team members to share their concerns without fear.

Example: Introduce an anonymous suggestion box or digital forum for team members to voice their concerns without attribution.

Impact: Encourages candid feedback and enhances communication without fear.

Long-Term Impact: Building and Sustaining Psychological Safety

1. Reward Constructive Behavior:

How to do this: Acknowledge and praise team members who exhibit the desired behaviors that contribute to a psychologically safe environment.

Example: Publicly recognize a team member who constructively challenged a proposed plan, highlighting the value of diverse thinking.

Impact: Reinforces positive behavior and promotes a culture of openness and challenge.

2. Offer Regular Training:

How to do this: Provide ongoing training in areas such as communication, conflict resolution, and inclusivity.

Example: Organize periodic workshops on effective communication and collaboration.

Impact: Builds conviction to the team members that whatever change you bring is really meant in true sense and it will increase the probability of one of them toward asking questions the next time when they have a doubt. When you start appreciating the ones who ask questions, it increases the likelihood of others to ask questions when they don't understand something.

ACTIVITIES

During a project kickoff meeting, you notice some team members seem hesitant to suggest creative solutions. What would you do?

- Stick strictly to the agenda to maintain meeting order.
- Pause the discussion to share a personal anecdote about a time your idea failed but led to learning, encouraging others to take risks.
- Continue without acknowledging the hesitation, focusing on completing the meeting as planned.

- Explicitly state, "I want to hear even the ideas that might seem out there. Often, these lead us to our most innovative solutions."

A team member respectfully challenges a long-standing process that they believe is outdated.

- Acknowledge their input but decide to continue with the current process without further discussion.
- Praise the team member for their courage to challenge the status quo and open a team discussion to explore potential improvements.
- Note their suggestions and say you will consider them without any follow-up.
- Privately tell the team members to align with the existing processes and avoid public challenges

Chapter 18

Rethinking Fear as a Motivator

As the nature of work evolves, our understanding of what motivates people in the workplace should also evolve. It's easy to assume that fear-based management still works, but in complex work environments that require collaboration and creativity, leading with fear is counterproductive.

Amy C. Edmondson, in her book "The Fearless Organization," explains:

Fear may have once acted to motivate assembly line workers on the factory floor or farm workers in the field - jobs that reward individual speed and accuracy in completing repetitive tasks. Most of us have been exposed to and internalized the figure of a villainous boss who rules by fear. Indeed, popular culture has exaggerated the stereotype to become comical, as in the animated Pixar film Ratatouille, where Remy, the rat, the story's cartoon hero, must first overcome the tyrannical restaurant chef who rules the kitchen if he is to realize his dream of becoming a chef.

Worse, many managers—both consciously and unconsciously—still believe in the power of fear to motivate. They assume that people who are afraid (of management or the consequences of underperforming) will work hard to avoid unpleasant consequences, and good things will happen. This might make sense if the work is straightforward and the worker is unlikely to run into any problems or have any ideas for improvement. However, for jobs where learning or collaboration is required for success, fear is not an effective motivator.

This chapter aims to provide managers with a nuanced understanding of implementing psychological safety in organizations, emphasizing why fear-based management not only fails to motivate but can actively hamper performance and well-being.

The Costs of Fear

Leading with fear creates an environment where employees are reluctant to speak up, share insights, or discuss potential issues. This lack of communication can have disastrous consequences, from code errors in software engineering to mishandling customer relations. Fear may seem to keep your team on their toes, but it can be a ticking time bomb, making your organization vulnerable to unexpected failures.

The Outdated Mechanics of Fear

It may seem like an intuitive management strategy to make employees a little fearful, as conventional wisdom suggests fear is a motivator for high performance. But times have changed. Unlike assembly line or farm work, most jobs today require intellectual engagement, creative problem-solving, and collaboration. In such settings, research shows that fear is a debilitating factor that diminishes these crucial abilities. Neuroscience further explains that fear activates the amygdala, a region in the brain that consumes physiological resources that would otherwise be used for analytical thinking, learning, and creative insight; for those who aren't conditioned to experience fear in professional settings, focusing on business challenges comes naturally. However, for individuals more susceptible to workplace anxieties, fear becomes a distraction that diverts attention from the tasks at hand. This isn't just detrimental to the individual but also to the collective potential of the team and organization. Even naturally confident people can find themselves uneasy in certain work environments, emphasizing the importance of a psychologically safe space for all. This is less likely a case in mechanical/assembly work because the tasks in such settings are often repetitive and don't require the same level of intellectual engagement or creative problem-solving. In assembly work, the primary focus is on speed and accuracy, which are tasks that can often be completed even when under some level of stress or fear. However, when your job requires you to think critically, collaborate with others, and be creative, fear becomes a major stumbling block. This is not to say that assembly workers or farm workers don't need psychological safety, but it makes a lot of difference for creative workers.

Fear-based environments can result in a host of negative consequences, such as:

1. **Information Hoarding:** Employees may be afraid to share crucial information with their team or higher-ups, worrying that they might be criticized or blamed.
2. **Reduced Innovation:** In a culture dominated by fear, employees are less likely to propose new, innovative ideas that could drive the organization forward.
3. **Lower Employee Satisfaction:** A stressful environment leads to lower job satisfaction, which can result in increased turnover rates.
4. **Poorer Quality of Work:** When employees are focused on the repercussions of making a mistake, they're not concentrating on doing their best work. The focus shifts from quality to simply "not messing up."

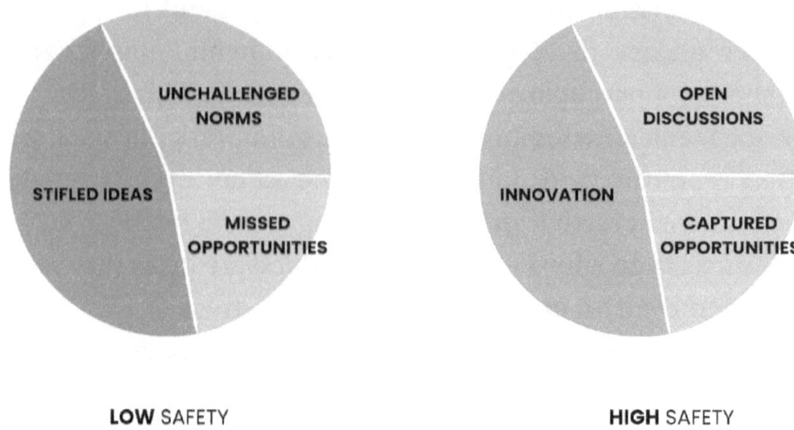

Takeaway

While it might seem tempting to rule with a firm hand and use fear as a motivator, such strategies are outdated and ineffective for modern work environments that depend on intellectual capital.

ACTIVITIES

As the new manager of a customer service department, you find that employees are hiding their mistakes for fear of being penalized, leading to unresolved customer issues and complaints.

- Introduce strict monitoring to track every employee's mistakes and enforce penalties more rigorously.
- Develop a mentorship program where more experienced employees work alongside less experienced ones to provide guidance and reduce the fear of making mistakes.
- Shift focus from penalizing mistakes to rewarding exemplary handling of customer issues, regardless of how many attempts it takes to resolve.
- Maintain current management practices but increase staff to handle potential customer complaints more effectively.

A new engineer on your team has opted out of a meeting, believing they may not be required to attend based on the company culture that encourages efficiency and self-directed participation in meetings.

- Commend their decision to manage time efficiently and encourage them to continue focusing on direct contributions.
- Explain the criteria for deciding when to attend meetings and ensure they understand the expectations for their participation.
- Direct them to attend all meetings initially for better integration and understanding of team dynamics.
- Ask why they felt the meeting was not useful and use this insight to improve the relevance of future meetings.

Chapter 19

Implementing Psychological Safety Across Different Types of Organizations

A Cautionary Tale

Imagine Company Dooolax, a tech firm eager to adopt agile methodology across all its teams. The upper management rolled out the change with great enthusiasm but minimal preparation. The resistance was swift and strong. Employees found the new methods confusing, supervisors found them hard to implement, and a general sense of chaos prevailed. It wasn't agile that was the problem; it was the lack of groundwork and psychological safety that led to its failure.

Just like agile or any other new approach, implementing psychological safety requires careful planning and a deep understanding of your organization's unique dynamics.

Understanding Organizational Dynamics

Every organization is unique, and there are different challenges to implementing psychological safety. Start-ups may struggle with setting professional boundaries, while larger corporations may find it challenging to foster trust amid bureaucratic layers. Identifying these challenges is crucial for overcoming them.

The Delicate Balance of Incentives

Misaligned incentives can be a significant roadblock. If upper management rewards only short-term gains, implementing a culture change for long-term benefits like psychological safety will be an uphill battle.

Beyond Zero-Sum Games

A zero-sum mentality, where one person's gain is seen as another's loss, often prevails in competitive environments. Embracing positive-sum games, where multiple parties can benefit, can help change this perspective.

A Framework for Implementation

1. Open Dialogue: Start by discussing psychological safety, its benefits, and how it aligns with your organization's values.
2. Pre-Mortem Analysis: Use this project management technique to forecast potential issues before they occur. It enables team members to express concerns without fear of ridicule.

Factors Affecting the Implementation of Psychological Safety

Organization Type/Size	Challenges	Prerequisites for Implementing it	How
Small Start-up	Limited Resources	Open Communication Channels	Active Listening Sessions, Regular Feedback Loops
Large Corporation	Bureaucracy	Leadership Buy-in	Psychological Safety Audits, Code of Conduct
Long-Tenured Employees	Resistance to Change	Reassurance of Job Security	Town-Hall Meetings, Storytelling Sessions
Short-Tenured Employees	Lack of Cohesion	Team Building Activities	Peer Recognition Programs, Training and Workshops
Flat Organization	Overlapping Roles	Clearly Defined Responsibilities	Regular Feedback Loops, "Two-Challenge Rule"
Hierarchical	Fear of Reprisals	Whistleblower Protection	Anonymous Suggestion Boxes, Psychological Safety Audits
Competitive Culture	Zero-Sum Mentality	Foster Collaboration	Training on Positive-Sum Games, Regular Feedback Loops
Collaborative Culture	Groupthink	Encourage Diverse Perspectives	"Two-Challenge Rule", Storytelling Sessions
Remote Teams	Isolation	Virtual Team-Building	Virtual Team Bonding Activities, Regular Check-ins
In-Person Teams	Physical Constraints	Adequate Meeting Spaces	In-Person Team Bonding Activities, Regular Check-ins

The Double-Edged Sword of Long Tenure

Long-tenured employees offer both stability and potential resistance to change. By communicating the value they bring and offering reassurance, they can be more willing to embrace change.

In conclusion, Psychological safety cannot be a one-size-fits-all solution. It requires a nuanced approach tailored to an organization's specific needs and challenges.

ACTIVITIES

You notice that fear of failure is preventing team members from innovating or trying new approaches to problem-solving.

- Introduce a 'failure forum' where team members can present their 'failures' and what they learned, normalizing, and learning from failure.
- Criticize failures in team meetings to underscore the importance of caution and precision in tasks.
- Only discuss successes in team settings to maintain a positive atmosphere.
- Establish a monthly review where failures are analyzed solely to identify responsible parties.

You are the director of an org where in the name of psychological safety, a manager insists that all communications be formalized and documented, which paradoxically makes team members less willing to speak up informally.

- Provide feedback that while documentation is important, the spirit of psychological safety also relies on spontaneous and open dialogue.
- Create informal communication channels such as weekly coffee meetings where team members can discuss their ideas and concerns in a relaxed setting.
- Enforce the formal communication policy more strictly, assuming that structure will eventually lead to openness.
- Host a session to redefine what psychological safety means, emphasizing that it should not lead to bureaucratic communication practices.

Chapter 20

Navigating Tradition and Risk: The Role of Pre-Mortem Analysis

The sinking of the Titanic Ship serves as a universal cautionary tale, teaching us the importance of considering negative outcomes. Titanic, which was considered to be non-sinkable during its launch, sank because it underestimated multiple factors, including the number of lifeboats, and never prepared for contingencies. There was no question of its safety.

Family and Community: Positive Cultural Frameworks

In the context of India, several cultural pillars provide a nurturing environment for individuals and families:

1. **Optimism as Emotional Resilience:** Being hopeful has been part of our upbringing, forming an emotional cushion for families to lean on.
2. **Careful Conversations:** Words are thought to carry a transformative power. Thus, conversations are often tailored to foster well-being.
3. **Unity in Diversity:** Navigating conversations to maintain social harmony has significant merit, especially within the microcosm of a family.

4. **Wisdom Across Generations:** Our respect for elders influences our life choices with the weight of generational wisdom.

These beliefs have proven their efficacy in our daily lives, fostering emotional strength and resilience within our family circles.

But these also hold us from asking tough questions with regards to worst-case scenarios when building a system which is used by several people.

From the Titanic to Modern Complexities: The Question of Scale

The Titanic engineers likely felt a strong sense of pride in their engineering marvel. However, the sinking of the ship highlighted the catastrophic impact of failing to consider worst-case scenarios. In today's India, where software systems power everything from critical public services to booming e-commerce platforms, the stakes are higher than ever. The code written by engineers aren't just lines of code; they are the neural pathways of our society, responsible for ensuring the well-being and convenience of millions. Given the scale and impact, rigorous scrutiny and contingency planning are not just best practices; they are ethical imperatives. Any oversight or failure in these systems could result in not just financial loss but, in extreme cases, jeopardize public welfare. Therefore, in the context of modern India's tech-driven organizations, adopting a culture that encourages post-mortem analysis and other risk-assessment techniques becomes non-negotiable.

Pre-mortem Analysis

There are numerous methods to carry out a pre-mortem analysis, each offering its unique set of advantages depending on the context and the team involved. However, the version that resonated with me the most is detailed by Shreyas Doshi in his enlightening article (https://medium.com/@shreyashere/how-to-use-pre-mortems-to-prevent-problems-blunders-and-disasters-6ecc6df6e22a).

In Shreyas' account, he captures not just the process but the underlying emotional shift that occurs when a team undertakes a pre-mortem:

After a well-run pre-mortem meeting, observe your team members as they exit the meeting. The odds are high that their faces will look more relieved, their gait more optimistic. Why? Because the problem that had been worrying them thus far is no longer just THEIR problem to carry. This catharsis can by itself be priceless.

While there are various ways to conduct a pre-mortem, the essence remains the same: creating an environment of psychological safety and collective responsibility. Particularly for those in India's tech sector, incorporating a methodology that enables team members to share openly can make a significant difference. It's not just about risk management; it's about creating a culture of openness, shared responsibility, and mutual respect.

Chapter 21

Avoiding Common Pitfalls: What Not to Do When Building Psychological Safety

Psychological safety requires nurturing and attention. While there are many things that leaders should do to foster this environment, it's equally important to recognize what not to do. Avoiding these pitfalls can prevent misunderstandings and ensure that your efforts to build a trusting and open team culture are successful.

1. Ignoring or Dismissing Ideas:

Impact: Causes frustration and disengagement and diminishes a sense of value within the team.

Example: An employee suggests a new approach in a team meeting and is met with silence or a dismissive response from leadership.

2. Punishing Mistakes:

Impact: Fosters a culture of fear and inhibits innovation and creativity.

Example: A team member makes an error on a project and is publicly reprimanded, leading others to become risk-averse.

3. Overloading with Unclear Expectations:

Impact: This leads to burnout and resentment and damages trust in leadership.

Example: A manager assigns a project with vague guidelines and an unrealistic deadline, causing stress and uncertainty.

4. Failing to Provide Constructive Feedback:

Impact: Hinders growth and development and creates confusion about performance standards.

Example: A leader providing only negative criticism without guidance on how to improve leaves the team members demotivated and unsure of how to proceed.

5. Creating a "Us Versus Them" Mentality:

Impact: Erodes team cohesion, leads to division and conflict within the organization.

Example: An executive makes disparaging remarks about another department, fostering a hostile environment and undermining collaboration.

6. Neglecting to Acknowledge Effort and Success:

Impact: Demoralizes the team and decreases motivation and satisfaction.

Example: Employees work extra hours to meet a tight deadline, and their efforts go unnoticed by leadership.

7. Withholding Information:

Impact: Causes mistrust and speculation and disrupts team dynamics and alignment.

Example: A manager knows about upcoming organizational changes but fails to communicate them, leading to rumors and uncertainty.

8. Requesting a Meeting Without an Agenda:

Impact: This creates confusion and anxiety, leading team members to wonder if something is wrong.

Example: A manager randomly asks a team member for a one-on-one meeting without context, leaving them to worry about potential issues or performance problems.

By recognizing and avoiding these common pitfalls, leaders can more effectively foster a psychologically safe environment where team members feel supported, valued, and empowered.

Chapter 22

Hurdles on the Road to Psychological Safety

Implementing psychological safety comes with its own set of challenges. It requires changes and transformations that might be difficult to adopt initially. However, acknowledging these challenges is the first step toward overcoming them.

1. **Cultural Barriers:** Cultural norms and values greatly influence an organization's behavior and attitudes. Changing deep-rooted cultural practices that discourage vulnerability and open communication can be a significant hurdle.

2. **Fear of Repercussions:** Employees may fear negative consequences if they speak up or disagree, leading to self-censorship and hindering psychological safety.

3. **Leadership Styles:** Traditional, authoritative leadership styles may not facilitate psychological safety. Leaders play a crucial role in creating a psychologically safe environment by encouraging open communication and showing vulnerability themselves.

4. **Lack of a Positive-Sum Game Mindset:** A zero-sum mindset, where one person's gain is seen as another's loss, can impede the development of psychological safety. Embracing a positive-sum mindset, where everyone can benefit, is crucial for building trust and encouraging open communication.

5. **Lack of Awareness and Understanding:** Sometimes, the challenge lies in the lack of awareness about what psychological safety is and why it's important. Unless the leaders understand its importance, they won't be motivated to create such an environment in their teams.

To overcome these barriers, it's crucial to cultivate an atmosphere that encourages open dialogue, shows empathy, and promotes a positive-sum game mindset. Organizations need to train their leaders to embrace these values and share them with their teams. Building psychological safety might be challenging, but the benefits it brings in terms of employee satisfaction, team performance, and overall organizational success are undoubtedly worth the effort.

Chapter 23

Self-Empowerment: Carving Paths of Personal Psychological Safety

Is the responsibility of providing psychological safety solely on the organization, or does it also lie with the individual?

To answer these questions, we must first acknowledge that organizations are entities composed of individuals, each with their unique circumstances, capacities, and challenges.

While it is indeed the organization's duty to create an environment that promotes psychological safety, individuals also play a crucial role in cultivating it. Change is a two-way street. If individuals take the initiative to foster psychological safety within themselves, even organizations that may not be aware or prepared to embrace such a culture will gradually and naturally adopt it. Let's be realistic— true change begins from within ourselves.

A Story:

At the core of an agile software start-up, three individuals—Ravi, Priya, and Aditya —demonstrate the power of personal transformation. Each of them took responsibility for fostering psychological safety within themselves, not solely relying on their organization.

Ravi, a Senior Engineer who is currently known for his assertiveness, started his journey in the challenging surroundings of Dharavi, Mumbai. Despite the meager income from his father's small tea shop, Ravi used his early experiences of hardship as motivation. He earned a scholarship to a prestigious college and took charge of his professional growth.

Instead of blaming his superiors when his ideas were dismissed, Ravi focused on expanding his horizons and diversifying his income sources. With a reliable financial fallback, he developed unconditional trust in himself, forming the foundation for his psychological safety.

Similarly, Priya, a Junior Engineer, applied the lessons she learned from her teacher and parents to her career. She invested time in strengthening her skills and achieving financial independence. Setting clear boundaries at work helped her avoid burnout and fostered a sense of safety and self-trust. This empowered her to confidently share her ideas and concerns.

Aditya, the VP of Engineering, came from a privileged background but faced his own struggles. A career burnout early on became his stepping stone toward self-improvement.

Aditya sought therapy, practiced mindfulness techniques, and embraced yoga to cope with the stress. These measures revitalized his mental health and instilled in him a deep sense of self-trust, which formed the bedrock of his psychological safety.

Ravi, Priya, and Aditya all took personal responsibility for fostering their own psychological safety. They developed unconditional self-trust, which strengthened their resilience and ability to express themselves without fear. Their journeys serve as a reminder that we have the power to shape our future by embracing self-responsibility, cultivating resilience, and nurturing self-trust. Through this inward journey, we can genuinely foster a deep-seated sense of psychological safety.

If you are looking for other ways to build psychological safety by yourself, follow amuldotexe in X/twitter (https://twitter.com/amuldotexe).

Here is one of the threads (https://x.com/amuldotexe/status/1605827859196416001?s=20) I like from this account.

Chapter 24

Psychological Safety – When Taken for Granted

Ravi Arumugam joined his first job as an Associate Software Engineer, fresh out of college at a small consultancy, TUC. The founder, Palaniappan, was committed to creating a supportive workplace for his team. After three years, Ravi moved to a different company and joined it with great enthusiasm.

However, Ravi faced challenges from the start. The frameworks he had learned in his previous job were not applicable here. But the issues ran deeper. At TUC, it was easy to ask for help; such behavior was encouraged. Regular meetings were organized to remind everyone that seeking help was okay if you lacked clarity.

In contrast, in his new organization, Ravi's questions often met with surprise.

"You have three years of experience, and yet you don't know this?"

This reaction was common whether he asked technical or business questions. When someone did offer help, they rushed through the information. Some seemed annoyed when Ravi asked further questions to understand the business objectives fully.

Ravi had learned that in 3 years, that it is not a good idea to start writing code right away without understanding the business objectives. Palaniappan always emphasized, "No code is good code." In his new environment, Ravi felt stifled, realizing that what he had taken for granted at the TUC couldn't even be imagined at his new company.

He reached out to his friends and ex-colleagues who had left TUC, discovering that most faced similar issues. Fortunately, some had supportive managers or teammates who offered help without judgment. Gathering courage, Ravi decided to call Palaniappan, wrestling with thoughts of potential negative reactions.

Would he be ridiculed? Dismissed?

During their conversation, Palaniappan inquired about Ravi's job and consoled him by saying, "This is the reality." Palaniappan had worked in multiple orgs as an Engineer for 30 years before starting TUC. That's when Ravi realized the value of what he had previously taken for granted.

Cases abound where individual managers or leaders protect their team's well-being from external pressures. Only the wise members recognize the importance of this safety and feel grateful for the protection. Others take it for granted and push the leaders to their limits, eventually leading to a reduction in benefits due to a lack of appreciation.

Psychological safety is essential for innovation but is a scarce resource in reality in Indian workplaces. Only with gratitude can we sustainably increase its influence. Entitlement prematurely depletes it.

We must value the managers and leaders who strive to provide psychological safety and reward them with gratitude and appreciation rather than taking their efforts for granted. Let us extend the benefits of psychological safety to everyone. Entitlement breaks the chain of good, but gratitude can extend it. Entitlement is easy. Gratitude is harder. Choose the harder one to progress.

Chapter 25

Psychological Safety – A New Competitive Edge and the Potential for Change

In a highly competitive global marketplace, businesses constantly strive to differentiate themselves. Traditionally, differentiation strategies focused on tangible elements such as product innovation, market penetration, or customer service. However, as our understanding of organizational success evolves, we are realizing the significant value of intangible factors, with psychological safety being paramount among them.

The compounding power of psychological safety is undeniable. It fosters a culture of innovation, improves productivity, reduces errors, and retains talent, creating an "ascending compounding effect" throughout the organization. Conversely, the absence of psychological safety can lead to a "descending compounding effect," characterized by limited innovation, decreased productivity, increased error rates, and talent attrition.

However, recognizing and implementing psychological safety remains challenging for many organizations. One significant obstacle is the intangible nature of psychological safety. It is like air - invisible yet vital. Its presence often goes unnoticed, but its absence can stifle an organization's potential.

What if organizations could leverage their commitment to psychological safety as a unique selling proposition (USP)? Imagine a world where companies are rated on their level of psychological safety, similar to the Environmental, Social, and Governance (ESG) ratings currently used. Such a system could serve as a reliable measure of an organization's dedication to creating a safe, inclusive, and nurturing work environment. This, in turn, could result in more reliable and consistent products or services, minimizing the risk of avoidable failures or oversights.

In this envisioned scenario, consumers would have the power to make informed choices, considering how the psychological well-being of their employees is taken care of. This shift in consumer behavior could drive businesses to foster environments rich in psychological safety, creating a positive, ascending compounding effect.

Nevertheless, it's crucial to acknowledge that while psychological safety is a key ingredient in an organization's success, it is not a standalone panacea. Just like how achieving CMMI Levels or other standards does not guarantee success, a high psychological safety rating doesn't ensure it either. Additionally, there is the potential for gaming the system, as with any ratings or certifications. (Goodhart's law) (https://sketchplanations.com/goodharts-law)

THE MISSING PIECE IN BUSINESS SUCCESS

In summary, the increasing complexity of our interconnected world makes psychological safety not just a desirable trait but a necessity. A psychological safety rating could provide a revolutionary competitive advantage, compelling businesses to adopt better practices and offering consumers a crucial deciding factor. After all, it is not only about offering the best product or service but doing so while prioritizing the psychological well-being of employees. As the adage goes, companies that take care of their employees also take care of their customers.

The Avianca Flight 052 Tragedy

Background

On January 25, 1990, Avianca Flight 052, a Boeing 707 aircraft, was flying from Colombia to New York's JFK Airport. What was supposed to be a routine international flight quickly turned into a grave disaster that would forever emphasize the importance of clear, assertive communication in high-stress environments.

Failure

As the aircraft approached its destination, it experienced a series of delays caused by heavy air traffic and challenging weather conditions. With fuel running low, the captain assigned the first officer with the important task of informing Air Traffic Control (ATC) about their critical fuel situation. However, the first officer made a fatal mistake by not explicitly declaring a 'fuel emergency.' Instead, they chose to request a 'priority landing' and mentioned that they were 'running out of fuel.' This unclear communication led to the ATC misunderstanding the severity of the situation. Tragically, Avianca Flight 052 crashed due to fuel exhaustion.

Surface Causes

The investigation conducted by the National Transportation Safety Board (NTSB) identified the following as the main reasons for the crash:

1. Fuel exhaustion

2. Inadequate communication of the flight crew regarding their fuel situation to ATC

Underlying Causes

Beneath these immediate causes, there were deeper cultural and psychological issues that contributed to the incident:

Fear of retribution: The first officer may have hesitated to communicate assertively due to fear of potential backlash.

Adherence to hierarchy: A culture of respect could have prevented the first officer from fully expressing the urgency of the situation.

The stress of the situation: The intense pressure of the circumstances may have inhibited the first officer's capacity for clear communication.

Cultural barriers: National, professional, or organizational norms might have led to the use of mitigated speech instead of clear and explicit communication.

Lack of psychological safety: The first officer perhaps did not feel psychologically safe to convey the crisis in a direct and unambiguous manner.

Therac-25

The Therac-25 was a radiation therapy machine developed by Atomic Energy of Canada Limited (AECL). In a tragic turn of events, the Therac-25 ended up delivering lethal doses of radiation to patients due to a software bug. This resulted in at least six known accidents that caused severe injuries and fatalities, leaving behind a haunting legacy.

Surface Level Causes:

1. Assumption-Based Development: The developers made a critical assumption that the software reused from the previous, safe models (Therac-6 and Therac-20) would function correctly on the new Therac-25 machine.

2. Lack of Hardware Safeguards: The Therac-25 lacked the hardware safety mechanisms present in the older models, which the team overlooked.

3. Insufficient Software Testing: The software was not thoroughly tested, and the developers assumed that it would function correctly based on its successful deployment in the older models.

4. Continued Use Despite Warnings: Even after initial incidents, the staff continued to administer radiation treatments using the Therac-25.

Underlying Causes:

1. Lack of Psychological Safety: The environment may not have encouraged questioning assumptions or challenging the status quo. Team members may have been afraid to speak up and express doubts about the reused software or the lack of hardware safeguards.

2. Communication Gaps: If there was better communication between the developers, product team, and administering staff, initial errors could have been identified and addressed earlier. This suggests a lack of a psychologically safe space preventing individuals from different teams felt comfortable voicing their concerns or providing feedback.

3. Fear of Admitting Mistakes: After the initial incidents, the continuation of treatments may have been due to the inability or fear to admit a serious mistake. This also indicates a lack of psychological safety, where admitting errors may have been perceived as a sign of weakness or incompetence.

On February 1, 2003, the Space Shuttle Columbia disintegrated upon re-entry into Earth's atmosphere, resulting in the tragic loss of all seven crew members: Rick D. Husband, William C. McCool, Michael P. Anderson, Ilan Ramon, Kalpana Chawla, David M. Brown, and Laurel B. Clark. This disaster highlighted severe organizational and cultural flaws within NASA, mirroring issues that had led to previous tragedies, such as the Challenger disaster.

Surface Level Causes:

Foam Impact Damage:

During launch, a piece of insulating foam from the external fuel tank struck Columbia's left wing, damaging the Thermal Protection System (TPS). This breach allowed superheated air to penetrate and melt the wing's aluminum structure during re-entry.

Inadequate Inspection and Repair Capability:

The Shuttle was not equipped with the means to thoroughly inspect and repair the damaged TPS while in orbit, which could have potentially prevented the catastrophe.

Flawed Safety Margins:

The design and testing processes underestimated the risks of foam strikes. Historical data on previous foam impacts were dismissed without thorough analysis or corrective actions.

Overconfident Risk Assessment:

NASA's risk assessment processes overly relied on past successes rather than incorporating rigorous testing and validation.

Underlying Causes:

Lack of Psychological Safety:

Organizational culture within NASA stifled the communication of safety concerns. Engineers and staff members did not feel empowered to voice their doubts or challenge the status quo, fearing reprisal or being ignored.

Communication Breakdowns:

Critical safety information was not effectively communicated across different levels of the organization. There was a failure to escalate the severity of the foam strike damage to the decision-makers who could have taken action.

Schedule Pressure:

Intense pressure to meet launch schedules and complete the International Space Station led to compromises in safety practices. The emphasis on adhering to timelines overshadowed the prioritization of thorough safety checks and risk assessments.

Normalization of Deviance:

Repeated exposure to minor anomalies, like foam strikes, without catastrophic outcomes led to a false sense of security. Deviations from safety norms became normalized, and the potential risks were underestimated.

Pressure to Protect NASA's Reputation:

There was significant pressure to maintain NASA's image and reputation, which contributed to downplaying safety concerns and risks. This pressure influenced decision-making processes, leading to the continuation of the mission despite known hazards.

Conclusion

The common thread across the incidents of Avianca Flight 052, Therac-25, and Space Shuttle Columbia is the lack of psychological safety, which prevented individuals from voicing critical concerns and hindered clear communication. These tragedies highlight the catastrophic consequences when fear, hierarchy, and cultural barriers suppress open dialogue.

In everyday office settings, while the stakes might not involve immediate life-or-death outcomes, the principles remain profoundly relevant. The absence of psychological safety can lead to withheld information, unreported errors, and stifled innovation, impacting the operational efficiency and creativity of a team. Over time, these issues can erode the foundation of a business, affecting its ability to adapt and thrive in competitive environments.

Moreover, workplaces devoid of psychological safety can contribute to employee stress and dissatisfaction, influencing not just professional but also personal lives. Employees take the stress home, affecting family dynamics and personal health. Conversely, when employees feel safe to express their ideas and concerns, they are more engaged and invested in their work. This not only enhances individual and team performance but also fosters loyalty and a positive organizational culture, which are critical for long-term business success.

Thus, cultivating psychological safety is essential not just for avoiding catastrophic failures but for tapping into the full potential of individuals and teams, leading to sustained growth and innovation in businesses. This strategic focus on psychological safety can transform potential risks into opportunities for development and progress.

Activities

1. **As a Manager, how can you ensure that all medical engineers feel responsible and empowered to report any faults in a medical equipment immediately?**

- Set up a clear, straightforward process for reporting equipment faults that bypass traditional bureaucratic hurdles.
- Hold regular safety briefings and workshops to reinforce the importance of vigilance and the procedures for reporting equipment issues.
- Introduce a cross-functional safety team that includes medical engineers, where discussions about equipment safety are routine.
- Offer protection for whistleblowers who report unsafe equipment, ensuring they do not face any form of retaliation.
- Encourage engineers to fix minor software bugs themselves without escalating to maintain efficiency.

2. **How would you create a culture where technical staff feel empowered to report potential flaws?**

- Warn staff that reporting flaws that turn out to be insignificant could harm their career progression.
- Offer assurances that there will be no negative consequences for reporting issues.

- Provide training on how to effectively communicate technical problems.
- Set up a dedicated team responsible for quality assurance and issue reporting.
- Regularly communicate the importance of transparency and safety in development.

3. **Your company culture has become highly competitive, leading to significant stress among employees. What steps would you take to alter this culture?**

- Continue promoting internal competition as a driver for performance, emphasizing that high stress is a part of the job.
- Introduce new policies that reward collaboration and team success rather than individual achievements.
- Organize team-building activities and workshops to improve communication and reduce competition.
- Conduct a survey to understand employee grievances and adjust the culture based on feedback.

4. **Considering the long-term investment needed to build a psychologically safe workplace, which strategy would be most effective?**

- Focus primarily on immediate business outcomes, viewing culture as a secondary concern.
- Develop a comprehensive program that includes training on psychological safety, regular feedback loops, and mechanisms for employees to voice concerns safely.
- Set clear metrics for psychological safety and include them in the performance evaluations of all managers.
- Encourage senior leaders to lead by example, openly discussing failures and vulnerabilities to foster an environment of trust and openness.

5. **Inspired by Toyota's Andon Cord system, how would you adapt this concept to suit a non-manufacturing environment to enhance psychological safety?**

- Decide it's not applicable to non-manufacturing environments and do not implement any similar system.
- Introduce a digital "Andon Cord" - a system where employees can raise concerns or suggest improvements through an internal app that notifies management instantly.
- Establish regular feedback loops where employees can voice concerns in a non-threatening environment, ensuring action is taken on valid inputs.
- Create a task force dedicated to identifying and addressing workplace issues, encouraging employees from all levels to participate.

6. **You discover that a lack of psychological safety is preventing your international branches from communicating effectively. What strategy would you employ to address this issue across cultural boundaries?**

- Enforce a uniform approach to communication and problem-solving across all branches, disregarding cultural differences.
- Customize psychological safety training that respects and incorporates different cultural norms and communication styles.
- Set up cross-cultural workshops that help employees understand and appreciate different perspectives and communication methods.
- Implement a global exchange program that allows employees from different branches to experience work in other cultural environments firsthand.

7. **A team member expresses regret after remaining silent about an idea that a competitor later successfully implemented. As their manager, how would you address their regret and encourage future contributions?**

- Tell them to move on and focus on current projects instead of dwelling on what could have been.
- Discuss what prevented them from sharing their idea previously and explore ways to mitigate these barriers going forward.
- Use this as a learning opportunity for the entire team, discussing the importance of sharing all ideas, regardless of how unformed they might feel.
- Encourage them to develop the next steps for any other ideas they might have, offering your support and resources to explore their potential.

8. **As a manager, how would you help a team member build confidence in their ideas and their ability to contribute meaningfully to the team?**

- Wait for them to gain confidence on their own through personal experience and success in smaller projects.
- Provide regular, constructive feedback on their contributions, highlighting both strengths and areas for growth.
- Pair them with a mentor who can guide them in developing and expressing their ideas more effectively.
- Set up regular check-ins to discuss their progress and any support they might need to feel more secure in their role.

9. **You notice that several team members hesitate to propose innovative solutions due to a fear of criticism or failure. What initiative might you introduce to cultivate a more supportive environment for innovation?**

- Maintain the current culture, prioritizing risk avoidance and sticking with proven methods.

- Introduce a "fail forward" award that celebrates risk-taking and learning from failed projects.
- Conduct workshops on the benefits of innovation and risk-taking, highlighting case studies from within the industry and your own company.

10. **Noticing increasing burnout signs among your team members, what strategies would you implement to ensure psychological safety while maintaining productivity?**

- Encourage longer work hours to keep up with demands, assuming that high performers can manage their stress levels.
- Implement flexible working hours and remote work options where feasible to allow employees to manage their work-life balance better.
- Introduce mandatory time-off policies and regular wellness workshops focusing on stress management and mental health.
- Offer a support program that includes access to mental health resources, regular check-ins, and a confidential counseling service.

11. **A team member repeatedly fails to meet deadlines, affecting team performance. Your team is psychologically safe, so how do you handle this situation without compromising that safety?**

- Avoid confronting the issue directly to not upset the team member.
- Have a private, supportive discussion with the team member about the impact of missed deadlines and explore solutions together.
- Publicly call out the behavior in a team meeting to make an example of the consequences of missing deadlines.
- Provide additional resources or support, assuming that the team member needs more help to meet expectations.

12. **In an engineering firm working on safety-critical systems, you learn that employees are reluctant to deliver bad news about project delays or potential safety issues. How do you address this to mitigate the Mum Effect?**

- Ignore the reluctance as a temporary issue, believing that critical problems will eventually be disclosed without intervention.
- Conduct anonymous surveys to gauge the extent of communication barriers and address them in a targeted manner.
- Hold workshops on the importance of transparency and the dangers of withholding information, especially in safety-critical contexts.
- Reassure the team that the sharing of bad news will be met with constructive responses and not punishment, possibly through policy changes.

13. **Some members of your team are skeptical about the benefits of psychological safety, preferring the familiarity of traditional work practices. How do you address this skepticism?**

- Dismiss the skeptics as resistant to change and focus only on those who are supportive.
- Organize workshops that provide evidence from research, like Google's Project Aristotle, highlighting the tangible benefits of psychological safety.
- Encourage a pilot project within one team to demonstrate the benefits of psychological safety, then share the results company-wide.
- Force rapid cultural shifts to quickly overcome skepticism, ignoring the need for gradual change and adaptation.

14. **You've noticed initial positive changes after introducing psychological safety measures, but you want to ensure**

these are not just short-lived. What strategies would you implement to sustain this change?

- Assume the initial success means the culture is permanently changed and reduce focus on psychological safety.
- Continually reinforce the value of psychological safety through regular leadership communication, success stories, and reinforcement of new norms.
- Periodically revise and update training programs to reflect new insights and feedback from the team.

15. **You are leading a diverse team where cultural differences sometimes lead to misunderstandings and conflict. How would you use psychological safety to improve team cohesion?**

- Ignore the cultural differences, expecting team members to resolve their issues independently.
- Conduct cultural sensitivity training and create forums for team members to express their perspectives and learn from each other.
- Enforce a standard communication style for everyone, disregarding cultural nuances.
- Encourage team-building activities that focus on sharing personal and cultural experiences, enhancing mutual understanding and trust.

16. **You want to cultivate a more inclusive environment where all team members feel comfortable sharing their ideas and concerns. Which strategy would best promote this type of psychological safety?**

- Establish an anonymous suggestion box that allows team members to voice concerns without fear of direct confrontation.
- Designate specific times during meetings for open floor discussions, encouraging everyone to contribute.

- Encourage senior team members to lead by example, sharing their own concerns and how they address them.
- Focus solely on efficiency and task completion, considering open communication as potentially distracting.

17. **You notice that during PR reviews, junior developers rarely provide feedback on the contributions of more senior team members, even when there are obvious issues or improvements that could be made.**

- Encourage junior developers in private to speak up more during reviews, without addressing the broader team dynamics.
- Organize a PR review workshop emphasizing the value of feedback from all levels and reiterating that respectful, constructive criticism is vital for growth and learning.
- Implement a rule where each PR must receive feedback from at least one junior and one senior developer before being approved.
- Overlook the lack of feedback, assuming that senior developers generally produce error-free code.

18. **A series of regression bugs were introduced in the latest release, causing critical disruptions. The team is quick to assign blame rather than focusing on solutions.**

- Hold a meeting to identify and reprimand the team members responsible for the oversight.
- Facilitate a blame-free retrospective that focuses on understanding the root causes of the regressions and developing strategies to prevent similar issues in the future.
- Ignore the blame game and direct all efforts solely toward fixing the bugs as quickly as possible.
- Introduce more stringent coding and review standards to prevent future errors without addressing the current conflict.

19. **A developer receives critical feedback on a PR that seems harsh and discourages them from contributing further. What would you do?**

- Address the feedback style in a team meeting to encourage more constructive and supportive communication.
- Ignore the incident, considering it a one-time issue.
- Privately coach the reviewer on how to provide feedback that is helpful and not harmful.
- Encourage the developer to respond defensively to justify their decisions.

20. **You are introducing pair programming in a team with diverse backgrounds, and some members are resistant due to fear of exposure or criticism.**

- Force all team members to participate immediately to accelerate the learning curve.
- Start with voluntary pair programming sessions, pairing willing participants first to demonstrate benefits.
- Hold a workshop to address fears and set expectations about the value of vulnerability and learning from each other.
- Ignore the resistance and expect team members to adjust on their own over time

Acknowledgment

This book would not be possible without these people. I have written this book with their support, inspiration and feedback and influence over my current lifetime.

Family
Parents: R.Selvaraj and S.Thilakavathi
In laws: A.Murugarasan and V.Pasupathy
Chitappa: E.Sivakumar
Periyappa: R.Ponnusamy

Colleagues/Friends/Mentors

1. Nils Nilsson - Product Manager
2. Amy C. Edmondson, Author, The Fearless Organization
3. Kumar Abhishek - Software Engineer
4. Murugesh T, Manager at Deloitte Consulting LLP
5. Nishant Mittal - Serial Entrepreneur, Founder @ Seneca
6. Ram Dhilip T - Data Engineer, National Cyber Security Center, Bahrain
7. Sathesh Premnath - Vice President & GM at SS&C Intralinks India

8. Mrinalini Sathesh Premath
9. Arun Prasad Rajkumar - Software Engineer at Timescale
10. Joseph Jude - CTO, Net Solutions
11. Shankar Ramamurthy, Partner, Effilor Consulting
12. Divya Raviraj, Mindset Coach
13. Prahalad Belavadi - Senior Software Engineer, Capital One
14. Gaurav Singh - Founder and Former CEO, 321 Educational Foundation
15. Viji Suresh - Co-Founder, Chief Operating Officer - Kartoffel Technologies
16. Ardian Mula - CEO, Foodhub
17. Nalin Chhajerr - Engineering Manager, Foodhub
18. Manjunath Chandrasekar - Director of Engineering, Best Buy
19. TamizhVendan S- Senior Technical Architect, Chargebee
20. Rajaraman Subramanian-Software Engineering Expert at Applied Materials
21. Lakshmanan Velayutham - Senior Director - Quality Engineering @ Tiger Analytics
22. Simon Sinek
23. Sridhar Vembu
24. Naval Ravikant
25. Shreyas Doshi

Books

The Fearless Organization: Creating Psychological Safety in the Workplace for Learning, Innovation, and Growth - Amy C. Edmondson

The Psychological Safety Playbook: Lead More Powerfully by Being More Human - Karolin Helbig (Author), Minette Norman (Author)

Videos

Workplace (https://www.youtube.com/watch?v=LhoLuui9gX8)

For Answers to activities

URL https://open.substack.com/pub/radhakrishnanselvaraj/p/silent-nods-lost-dollars-activities?r=4156p&utm_campaign=post&utm_medium=web&showWelcomeOnShare=true

Subscribe to my Newsletter

https://radhakrishnanselvaraj.substack.com/

Author Bio

Radhakrishnan S is a Senior Software engineer with a career spanning 15 years. Drawing from rich experiences in the tech industry, his book offers insights into building a workplace where trust and efficiency coexist harmoniously. His passion is in writing about the synergy between psychological safety, trust, collaboration, learning, and acknowledging vulnerabilities, contributing to a robust organizational culture. Beyond his technical work, Radhakrishnan cherishes mentoring with First Principles thinking, storytelling, drawing inspiration from everyday news to weave narratives. He enjoys playing with his son, constructing small structures with wooden blocks and tinkering with Arduino cars.

Notes